GORILLA LAWFAIR

A PRO SE LITIGATION MANUAL

VOLUME I

ANPU UNNEFER AMEN

© Copyright 2014 Anpu Unnefer Amen.

All rights reserved. No part of this publication may be reproduced, stored in a retrieval system, or transmitted, in any form or by any means, electronic, mechanical, photocopying, recording, or otherwise, without the written prior permission of the author.

Printed in the United States of America.

ISBN: 978-1502902764

Because of the dynamic nature of the Internet, any web addresses or links contained in this book may have changed since publication and may no longer be valid. The views expressed in this work are solely those of the author and do not necessarily reflect the views of the publisher, and the publisher hereby disclaims any responsibility for them.

Any people depicted in stock imagery provided by Thinkstock are models, and such images are being used for illustrative purposes only.
Certain stock imagery © Thinkstock.

CONTENTS

Disclaimer ix
Dedications xi
Preface xiii
Criminal Activity xv
Acknowledgements xvii
Foreword xix
Introduction 1
    A Brief Introduction To Criminal Law 1
    Arrest 2
    U.S. Supreme Court 7
    Miranda Revisited 7
    Booking 10
    Line-Ups 11
    Pre-Arraignment Interview 11
    Assigned Counsel 12
Grand Juries 15
    Grand Jury Proceedings 15

Postconviction Remedies	19
Where To File A 440 Motion	23
When To File	23
What To File	24
Where To File	25
What To Expect After You File	25
Sample 440.10 Motion	26
Sample Letter	71
Blank 440.10 Motion	73
Sample 440.20 Motion	79
Blank 440.20 Motion	93
Writ Of Error Coram Nobis	98
Where To File A Coram Nobis Petition	99
What To File	99
What To Expect After You File	100
Appellate Court Addresses	101
Sample Writ Of Error Coram Nobis	102
Blank Writ Of Error Coram Nobis	130
28 U.s.c. §2241 Motions For Habeas Corpus	145
Where To File A §2241 Petition	147
What To File	147
What To Expect After You File	148
Sample Letter	150
Sample Writ of Habeas Corpus	165

PAROLE 183
    Parole Defined 183
    Parole and Corrections 184
    Parole Law Changes 184
    Parole Memo 188
    Transitional Accountability Plan 189
    Assembly Corrections Committee 190
    COMPAS 191
    Professor Phillip M. Genty 192
    The Thwaites Case 193
    Directive #4803 194
    Preparing For The Parole Board 196
    COMPAS Re-Entry Assessment 198
    Risk and Needs Assessment 200
    Crime Victims 201
    Parole Packages 202
    Appealing Final Parole Board Decisions 205
    Sample Administrative Parole Appeal 208
Article 78 Proceedings 223
    Exhausting Your Remedies 224
    Questions Raised 224
    Where To File An Article 78 227
    What To File 227
    What To Expect After You File 229

Sample Article 78 231
Appealing An Article 78 Decision 248
Blank Article 78 Appeal 251
Sample Article 78 Appellate Brief....................................260
The Court Of Appeals..287
Appeals To The Court Of Appeals As Of Right................289
Motions For Leave To Appeal 291
Which Court? 291
When To File 291
What To File 291
Motions For Leave To Appeal 291
Criminal Leave Applications..291
Civil Leave Applications 292
What To Expect After You File 293
Sample Leave To Appeal Motion 295

DISCLAIMER: IMPORTANT INFORMATION REGARDING THIS BOOK

—PLEASE READ!

GORILLA LAWFAIR Is sold without guarantees or warranties of any kind, express or implied, and the author and publisher disclaim any liability, loss or damages caused by the contents of **GORILLA LAWFAIR.**

GORILLA LAWFAIR does not intend or purport to take the place of expert legal advice that should be provided by an attorney. Before filing any legal documents with the Court, the readers of **GORILLA LAWFAIR** are strongly recommended to seek the assistance of a competent licensed attorney before filing any legal documents in any Court in order that they may avoid any potential risks often inherent in the legal system that can result in negative consequences.

GORILLA LAWFAIR is inclusive of information assumed to be from reliable sources. The constitutional laws, legislative laws, and case law referred to in this book are current as of August 2011. The Sample Forms and Blank Forms that are in this manual are intended to provide insight into the type of information that may be required in a particular type of legal filing. However, all forms and legal documents filed in a particular Court of law should be in compliance with the type of that particular Court or meet that particular Court's rules and procedures.

Due to the constant changes in the law, all statutes, rules and regulations, guidelines and case law cited in **GORILLA LAWFAIR** should be checked and updated to ensure their accuracy before being relied upon as sound by **GORILLA LAWFAIR** readers.

THE SHRINE OF KHPRA
414 Marcus Garvey Blvd.
Brooklyn, NY 11233
347-737-1942
Gorillalawfair.com

DEDICATIONS

To My Queen Nefert Amen May the Creator and the Ancestors continue to guide you and allow your Light to Shine...

To Shaquana and Lateef, Stephanie, Jasmin, Jamar, and Eunice... You are all our future!

To Beatrice "Glady's" Taylor, Anna Louise Simons, Rose Waters, Patricia Watson, and Jacqueline Scott...

--Rest In Peace!

To our Brotha Born. Our prayers are with you... R.I.P.!

PREFACE

Most of the legal situations referenced in the Sample Motions in this book are only a fraction of those that incarcerated individuals are often confronted with. In the 21st Century with all of the budget cuts throughout the nation's correctional departments and other governmental agencies, even the non-profit organizations that once aided prisoners with their legal issues have either went into oblivion or have limited their services to certain issues due to budget constraints and shortage of staff. With the abolition of federally funded college programs in prisons and the growing shortage of legal research programs, there has been a steady growth in the number of people being illegally held in prisons throughout America. This text provides various forms, letters, legal arguments, and explanations of the law to give readers who are not familiar with the law and those who are, insight into some of the issues affecting individuals who usually have no voice or the legal knowledge to champion their own cause.

This book, GORILLA LAWFAIR: A PRO SE LITIGATION MANUAL, is written for anyone interested in a text which provides different approaches to litigating issues that most paralegals in society will probably never encounter.

CRIMINAL ACTIVITY

Crimes and criminal activity exist throughout our neighborhoods, and those who commit these acts are usually unaware of the lasting effects that their actions really have upon their communities and society as a whole. Many of our youths have gravitated towards gangs, drugs, promiscuity, and violence. The end result of which is almost always prison or death! Maybe if they knew what kinds of penalties they faced if they were caught it would serve as a deterrent? Wrong answer!!! Consequences have never served as a deterrent to the commission of crimes and it never will! Only the changing of morals and values can change criminal behavior.

ACKNOWLEDGEMENTS

The work and understanding that went into the making of this text book took several years to get to this point. Through the legal knowledge that was imparted by William "Khalil" Cromwell, Muhammad Faruq, Bruce Maddox, and Ralph Popkins, Esq., a strong foundation leading up to this kind of book was laid; Pop and Stew from Blackstar Music & Video in Harlem for making our first edition available on blackstarvideo.com, Straight Stuntin, F.E.D.S., and Sweets Magazines; The Coalition for Parole Restoration; Judith Brink and Prison Action Network for their support; Charlie & Pauline Sullivan and the various chapters of National CURE; the Pennsylvania Prison Society; Janine Morna and the Jailhouse Lawyer's staff at Columbia University for allowing us to utilize some of your material for Volume II; Professor Phillip M. Genty of Columbia University for your insight on the current issues regarding parole; Adam "House" Adams for your Foreword to Volume II; to our Brothers Courtney Muhammad and Ronald Muhammad whose Prison Ministry work on behalf of the Nation of Islam and the Honorable Minister Louis Farrakhan transcends the prison walls; We are also grateful to Robert Seth Hayes and Herman Bell. Two political prisoners who are very decent human beings with a strong sense of humanity that could benefit the world if given the opportunity; We would also like to shout out Roland "Zulu" Cody, Shabaka Shakur, Nate

Lewis, Darryl Kenyatta Morgan, Ausar Unnefer Amen, Lil Wag, Big S, Arthur Brodie, Paul McKay, and Thomas Cross for staying real and committed to the liberation struggle.

A very special thanks to our artist Christopher "Cipher" Garcia. That Gorilla you drew for the cover is official; to Leon "Peewee" Watson Jr., Kimberly Renee Watson, and Raymond Watson; To our Sista-Queen Muqita Lumumba who raised the bar by saying it could be done; Andre "Knowledge" Waters, welcome home!; to our Brotha Damon "Nu-Nu" Chance, thanks for all your support. Robert "Poo" Chance (R.I.P.); Tyrone "T-Rock" Baum (R.I.P.), and Darryl "Hommo" Baum (R.I.P); Barron "Unique" Sanders (R.I.P.); Frederick "Chase" Dickson (R.I.P.); to Shaborn, and Miz, "L.G. Rock On!"; To Derrick "Bush" Hamilton, welcome home and thank you for your assistance with this revision and the introduction to Volume II.

Further, we would like to recognize all of the Warrior Queens who go through the extra lengths to show their love and loyalty to the brothas and sistas on lockdown throughout the universe; to Brooklyn Senator Velmanette Montgomery and the role you play in struggling to keep it fair across the board; and to the Sistas on lockdown, our hearts go out to you. We trust that some of you will read something in this book that will help to serve as a key to your freedom; Para mi familia latinos y latinas, LIBERTAD! Siga la pelea; Pedro "Caballo" Nunez (R.I.P.); T-45 (R.I.P.) ; Leonilda "Yunito" Sierra, we wish you the best in your situation bro!; To Wayne-0 and Deb -- "Free The People!: To Baba Heru Ur and The Shrine of Khpra, Hotep! Thank you for making this project possible!

If we forgot to mention you it was by mistake! In real life! LOVE IS LOVE!!!

GORILLA LAWFAIR.
2nd Edition

FOREWORD

As I sit on this uncompromising steel bed in one of the 71 prisons in the New York State Correctional System writing the foreword to Gorilla Lawfair and contemplate, all sorts of thoughts come to mind. What has inspired me to write is the many conversations I have had with a very good friend that I have known since 1988. 1988 happens to be the year that I came to prison. According to the Bureau of Justice Statistics, there is a 67.5% recidivism rate in the United States. Unfortunately, I have not had the opportunity to be freed like most people in this place. My maximum sentence is life!

My good friend that I was talking about is the author of Gorilla Lawfair: A Pro Se Litigation Manual Volumes I and II. Most people don't take advantage of the knowledge that is available to them or the many things that they learn in these facilities. Mr. Anpu Amen is a man whom fighting for his own freedom found that the law could assist others in getting out. The biggest problem for men and women of all nationalities in this system is that most of us do not know how to read law. More often times than not, we do not seek help because when we do seek help our experience is that people are usually trying to play predator and make a fast buck off of us, or seeking to provide information to the district attorney's office in exchange for a lighter sentence.

Incarcerated individuals aren't in the habit of telling their people about the countless ills that occur in these places. Such as how everyone in these prisons aren't guilty of a crime, but because the majority don't have the money or the know how to litigate, they somehow get caught up in a system that acts as the authority for a society whose power is dwindling. The systems laws and rules are supposed to apply equally to all which isn't the case often enough. So when a book such as Gorilla Lawfair comes around, it gives families comfort knowing that there is something around that can potentially aid their incarcerated family members with assistance in handling some of the complex issues they may encounter. With a rate of 1 out of every 136 adults incarcerated, the United States is the leader when it comes to incarcerating its citizens! 5 out of 10 young men have either been incarcerated or are on parole or probation.

In most cases, incarcerated individuals are the only ones who can teach other incarcerated individuals. In other cases it is left up to the ministers of the different faiths. In addition to this, only real brothers and sisters who come together can teach the younger people within the system the mandated programs that the Parole Board panels no longer seem to respect. These programs aren't attractive to the younger population because they feel that they are being forced into programs that are useless. In 1999, Governor Pataki introduced determinate sentences that are commonly called "flat bids." Correctional Unions praised him for it, and numerous government officials gave him their support. However, truth be told, it made the correctional system in New York State worse because a large amount of the people sentenced to the determinate sentences feel that they have nothing to lose. For instance, an individual with a determinate sentence of 5 years knows that they can be released within 4 years and 3 months if they take all of the mandated programs and maintain a clean disciplinary record. They also know that the worst case scenario is that the system will have to release them after serving a maximum of 5 years irregardless of whether they have a poor disciplinary and refuse to program. This negative attitude results in many long term incarcerated individuals receiving a deuce (two years) at the Parole Board to balance the numbers.

After being incarcerated during the terms of four governors, I have literally observed the state and this system go down the drain. Government officials claim that they are trying to give the government back to the people. But what about their family members that have been railroaded into the system, or have served more than enough time? When will they give them back to their people? The struggle continues.

—Adam Lee Adams

INTRODUCTION

A BRIEF INTRODUCTION TO CRIMINAL LAW

Criminal law as we know it today has evolved from laws that were in existence from time immemorial. In Kemet, or Egypt, there were the 42 fundamental laws out of 147 that individuals had to be able to come in harmony with and be able to recite. They are known as the "admonitions of Maat." After Moses became educated in the Egyptian Temples he is said to have inscribed some of these laws on stone tablets. Today they are called the "Ten Commandments." The Greeks, who were also taught by the Egyptians established laws that were later adopted and expanded upon by the Romans.

In England, the Magna Carta was established in 1215 and eventually was utilized as the foundation of the United States Constitution. The right to a trial by jury, the right against self-incrimination, the right against illegal searches and seizures, the right to confrontation, and others were integrated into the U.S. Constitution and are still considered "bedrock" principles.

The United States Government is comprised of three different branches, i.e., legislative, executive and judiciary. These three branches are delegated with certain powers that created what is called "checks and balances" within the system. Laws are enacted by legislative bodies. On a federal level laws are enacted by the United States Congress and signed by the President, who is a member of the executive branch. State laws are enacted by State legislatures and are signed by the Governor, who is a member of the executive branch on a State level. Judges and the Court system make up the judicial branch of government. The United States Constitution is the "supreme law of the land," and the United States Supreme Court has the final say as to whether particular actions or laws are in conformity with, or in violation of the Constitution. Article 6, clause 2 of the U.S. Constitution, which is known as the "Supremacy Clause," makes the U.S. Constitution and its interpretation by the U.S. Supreme Court the "supreme law of the land."

As far as crimes go, it is often stated that the majority of crimes are committed by "poor, uneducated young males." The different classes of crimes are violations, misdemeanors, and felonies. Violations are non-criminal offenses that usually result in fines, such as traffic violations. Misdemeanor crimes are less serious than felonies and carry sentences from a few days to a year upon conviction. Felonies are crimes that can carry anywhere from a year up to the death penalty depending on the severity of the offense.

ARREST

> "I do not wish to answer any questions without speaking to an attorney first. I do not consent to a search of my home, my car or my person. I also do not consent to being in a line-up or a show-up. I will not waive any of my constitutional rights under any circumstances."

If you are arrested and accused of committing a crime the best thing you can do at that point is "keep your mouth shut!" In the landmark case Miranda v. Arizona, the U.S. Supreme Court ruled that :

> "when an individual is taken into custody or otherwise deprived of his freedom by the authorities in any

significant way and is subject to questioning, the privilege against self-incrimination is jeopardized. Procedural safeguards must be employed to protect the privilege, and unless other fully effective means are adopted to notify the person of his right to silence and to assure that the exercise of that right will be scrupulously honored, the following measures are required. He must be warned prior to any questioning that he has the right to remain silent, that anything he says can be used against him in a court of law, that he has the right to the presence of an attorney, and that if he cannot afford an attorney one will be appointed for him prior to any questioning if he so desires. Opportunity to exercise these rights must be afforded him throughout the interrogation. After such warnings have been given, and such opportunity afforded him, the individual may knowingly and intelligently waive these rights and agree to answer the questions or make a statement."

In 2010, the United States Supreme Court issued a decision in the case of Berghuis, Warden v. Thompkins, 560 U.S. _____, 130 S.Ct. 2250, regarding the right to remain silent that made significant changes to the Fifth Amendment guarantee. On January 10, 2000, two people were shot outside of a mall in Southfield, Michigan. One of the victims died, and the other victim survived. The surviving victim identified Van Chester Thompkins as a suspect in the crime. Mr. Thompkins left Michigan and became a fugitive of justice.

Approximately one year later, Mr. Thompkins was apprehended in the state of Ohio. Two police officers from Michigan travelled to Ohio and interrogated Mr. Thompkins for about three hours in a small 8 by 10 feet room. One of the officers presented Mr. Thompkins with a form that was rooted in the landmark case Miranda v. Arizona, apprising him of his Fifth Amendment right to remain silent. The form read:

"NOTIFICATION OF CONSTITUTIONAL RIGHTS AND STATEMENT"

"1. You have the right to remain silent.

"2. Anything you say can and will be used against you in a court of law.

"3. You have the right to talk to a lawyer before answering any questions and you have the right to have a lawyer present with you while you are answering any questions.

"4. If you cannot afford to hire a lawyer, one will be appointed to represent you before any questioning, if you wish one.

"5. You have the right to decide at any time before or during questioning to use your right to remain silent and your right to talk with a lawyer while you are being questioned."

Mr. Thompkins was asked to read all of the Miranda warnings and then sign the form. Mr. Thompkins refused to sign the form, and according to the officers, Mr. Thompkins never expressed that he wanted an attorney, that he wanted to remain silent, and that he didn't wish to talk to the officers.

According to one of the officers, after almost three hours of questioning he asked Mr. Thompkins, "Do you believe in God?" To which Mr. Thompkins replied "Yes." The officer said he then asked Mr. Thompkins "Do you pray to God?" To which he is alleged to have said "Yes." The final and most damaging part of this exchange occurred when Mr. Thompkins was asked "Do you pray to God to forgive you for shooting that boy down?" And he replied "Yes."

Mr. Thompkins never made a written confession, however, he was charged with first degree murder, assault with intent to commit murder, and certain firearms-related offenses. During the hearing to suppress his statements, Mr. Thompkins' attorney argued that he had exercised his Fifth Amendment right to remain silent which required the officers to abruptly end their interrogation of him. The trial judge disagreed with this argument and denied their motion to suppress Thompkins' statements as being involuntarily made and in violation of his Fifth Amendment right to remain silent. See Michigan v. Mosley, 423 U.S. 96, 103 (1975) quoting Miranda v. Arizona, 384 U.S. 436 at 474.

During trial, the prosecutor's theory was that Mr. Thompkins shot the victims from the passenger seat of a van which was driven by Eric Purifoy. Mr. Purifoy had been previously charged for the shooting under the pretense that he aided and abetted Mr. Thompkins by being the driver of the vehicle that Mr. Thompkins allegedly did the shooting from. Mr. Purifoy was acquitted of murder and assault, and was convicted of weapons charges.

Mr. Purifoy testified that he was indeed driving the van when the shooting occurred and that Mr. Thompkins was in the passenger seat, but he added another person named Myzell Woodward to the crime by stating that he was in the van as well. He further stated that when the shooting occurred he was bending down close to the floor so he never saw who did the actual shooting. After the shooting, Mr. Purifoy said that Mr. Thompkins told him "What the hell are you doing? Pull off," and it was then that he noticed that Mr. Thompkins happened to be holding a pistol as he drove away.

To complicate matters further, letters that Mr. Purifoy had sent to Mr. Thompkins were introduced at Mr. Thompkins' trial that he wrote in an effort to prove that he did not "snitch" or "rat" on Mr. Thompkins, and that they were both innocent of the shootings.

At the conclusion of the trial during the closing arguments, the prosecution implied that Mr. Purifoy lied about not seeing Mr. Thompkins shoot the victims:

"Did Eric Purifoy's Jury make the right decision? I'm not here to judge that. You are not bound by what his jury found. Take his testimony for what it was, [a] twisted attempt to help not just an acquaintance but his tight buddy."

Defense counsel for Mr. Thompkins did not object to the prosecutor's statement, nor did they ask the Judge for an instruction limiting the jury's consideration of the prosecutor's statement to the assessment of Mr. Purifoy's credibility, rather than the establishment of Mr. Thompkins' guilt or innocence.

When the verdict was handed down, Mr. Thompkins was found guilty of every count in the indictment. At sentencing he was given a sentence of life in prison without the possibility of parole. His subsequent motions for a new trial filed by his appellate lawyer, and his postconviction motion alleging ineffective assistance of counsel were also denied.

After unsuccessfully challenging his conviction on a state appellate level and in the United States District Court for the Eastern District of Michigan, Mr. Thompkins received a favorable ruling in the United States Court of Appeals for the Sixth Circuit. 547 F.3d 572.

In its. ruling, the Court of Appeals ruled that the state court made an unreasonable determination of the facts because "Thompkins's persistent silence for nearly three hours in response to questioning and repeated invitations to tell his side of the story offered a clear and unequivocal message to the officers: Thompkins did not wish to waive his rights."

Secondly, the Court of Appeals reasoned that "because Thompkins's central strategy was to pin the blame on Purifoy, there was a reasonable probability that the result of Thompkins's trial would have been different if there had been a limiting instruction regarding Purifoy's acquittal."

U.S. SUPREME COURT

The U.S. Supreme Court granted certiorari in the case to render a final disposition of the issues according to the Antiterrorism and Effective Death Penalty Act of 1996 (AEDPA), that was signed into law by President Bill Clinton. Under the standard enunciated in 28 U.S.C. §2254(d), federal courts cannot grant federal habeas corpus petitions "with respect to any claim that was adjudicated on the merits in state court proceedings," unless the respective states' lower court decision "was contrary to, or involved an unreasonable application of clearly established Federal law, as determined by the Supreme Court of the United States," §2254(d)(1), or "was based on an unreasonable determination of the facts in light of the evidence presented in the State court proceeding, §2254(d)(2)."

MIRANDA REVISITED

In order to properly assess whether Mr. Thompkins' Fifth Amendment rights were violated it was necessary for the court to revisit Miranda v. Arizona to see if the warning he was given was consistent with that of Miranda:

> "He must be warned prior to any questioning that he has the right to remain silent, that anything he says can be used against him in a court of law, that he has the right to the presence of an attorney, and that if he cannot afford an attorney one will be appointed for him prior to any questioning if he so desires."

Although Thompkins's attorney alleged that his silence should have been viewed as an invocation of his right to remain silent, the Supreme Court, citing Davis v. United States, 512 U.S. 452, 459 (1994), rejected their argument and ruled that: "If an accused makes a statement concerning the right to counsel 'that is ambiguous or equivocal' or makes no statement, the police are not required to end the interrogation, ibid., or ask questions to clarify whether the accused wants to invoke his or her Miranda rights."

The ramifications of this decision are spelled out by Justice Sotomayor who delivered the decision of herself and the other three Justices who disagreed (dissented) with the majority's decision:

> "The Court concludes today that a criminal suspect waives his right to remain silent if, after sitting tacit and uncommunicative through nearly three hours of police interrogation, he utters a few one-word responses. The Court also concludes that a suspect who wishes to guard his right to remain silent against such a finding of "waiver" must, counterintuitively speak-and must do so with sufficient precision to satisfy a clear-statement rule that construes ambiguity in favor of the police. Both propositions mark a substantial retreat from the protection against compelled self-incrimination that Miranda v. Arizona, 384 U.S. 436 (1966), has long provided during custodial interrogation."

She went on further to state that:

> "Today's decision thus ignores the important interests Miranda safeguards. The underlying constitutional guarantee against self-incrimination reflects 'many of our fundamental values and most noble aspirations,' our

society's 'preference for an accusatorial rather than an inquisitorial system of criminal justice'; a 'fear that self-incriminating statements will be elicited by inhumane treatment and abuses' and a realization that while the privilege is 'sometimes a shelter to the guilty, [it] is often a protection to the innocent.' Withrow v. Williams, 507 U.S. 680, 692 (1993) (internal quotation marks omitted). For these reasons, we have observed, a criminal law system 'which comes to depend on the 'confession' will, in the long run, be less reliable and more subject to abuses than a system relying on independent investigation.' Ibid. (some internal quotation marks omitted). 'By bracing against 'the possibility of unreliable statements in every instance of in-custody interrogation,' 'Miranda's prophylactic rules serve to 'protect the fairness of the trial itself.' 507 U.S., at 692 (quoting Johnson v. New Jersey, 384 U.S. 719, 730 (1966); Schneckloth v. Bustamonte, 412 U.S. 218, 240 (1973). Today's decision bodes poorly for the fundamental principles that Miranda protects."

She concluded her dissent by stating:

"Today's decision turns Miranda upside down. Criminal suspects must now unambiguously invoke their right to remain silent--which, counterintuitively, requires them to speak. At the same time, suspects will be legally presumed to have waived their rights even if they have given no clear expression of their intent to do so. Those results, in my view, find no basis in Miranda or our subsequent cases and are inconsistent with the fair-trial principles on which those principles are grounded. Today's broad new rules are all the more unfortunate because they are unnecessary to the disposition of the case before us."

This represents a major turning point from the original Miranda decision because it dictates that an accused has to clearly state to the police that they wish to exercise their right to counsel and their right to remain silent before their right to remain silent will be recognized in a court of law. At the same time, an accused must also "keep their mouth shut" afterwards or run the risk of having whatever they say used against them irrespective of their having invoked their right to remain silent. A great deal of individuals who are accused of a crime that try to slick talk their way out of it usually find out later that it would have served them some justice to be quiet. Also, that they shouldn't have spoken to other people who were locked up with them about their crime because they were the same people who testified against them later. Individuals who are arrested shouldn't go into the particulars of their crime when they make their phone calls or make any signed or verbal statements.

BOOKING

When a person suspected of committing a crime is booked, they are asked basic background information such as their name, date of birth, address and etc. They are also fingerprinted and photographed. They will also be searched and have to turn over their personal property for safekeeping. The authorities will issue a voucher for the property. In some cases, where the offense is not that serious the individual can be issued a desk appearance ticket and released in their own recognizance (ROR) from the precinct with the understanding that they are to appear in court on a specified date for their initial appearance. In most cases they will have to await transportation to central booking and wait until the arresting officer and the district attorney's office decide which charges are going to be brought forth, if any.

LINE-UPS

If you are arrested for a crime that requires that you be identified by the victim or a witness, you will either be placed in a line-up, or the police will try to put you in a show-up. The difference between the two is that in a show-up identification the crime victim will be brought to you wherever you are and asked if you are the person who violated them. More than likely you will be in the police car or at the precinct in a holding cell with handcuffs on. Under those circumstances you might be picked out even if you aren't the person who perpetrated the crime against them. Never consent to being placed in a show-up or a line-up. Always tell the police that you want a lawyer.

A line-up is conducted by putting other individuals in a room with you that usually don't resemble you and have you sit in a row holding a number. The other individuals in the line-up are called fillers. The victims of the crime and/or witnesses are then asked to look through a one-way mirror to see if there is anyone that they recognize. If they pick you out it will make the case against you appear strong. It's best to have a lawyer there for you in this process because they can be there to try to ensure that the process is done fairly. The police usually take a photo of the suspect and the fillers in the line-up to be used in future court proceedings. However, once the photo is copied it will be difficult to show that the other people in the black and white copy don't resemble you at all.

PRE-ARRAIGNMENT INTERVIEW

Prior to being arraigned on the charges, individuals in New York will be interviewed by the Criminal Justice Agency. Those in Federal custody will be interviewed by Pre-Trial Services. The purpose of these interviews is to possibly place those accused of committing a crime in a better position of being released in their own recognizance or receiving the lowest possible bail. The questions they ask will revolve around an individual's criminal record (if any), their residence (where they live), and their employment (where they currently work). They will also ask if the individual is married, if they have children, and whether they have someone who can be contacted to verify the information being given to them. If they find out that the information being provided is unreliable it will not look good in front of the judge deciding whether to grant release, set bail, or keep the individual in custody.

ASSIGNED COUNSEL

Individuals who are accused of crimes and cannot afford to pay for an attorney to represent them are guaranteed the right to counsel under the Sixth Amendment to the United States Constitution. This right was established in 1963 by the United States Supreme Court in the case of Gideon v. Wainright, 372 U.S. 335, 83 S.Ct. 792.

Before an individual makes their initial appearance in Court, if they do not have a paid attorney there to represent them, one will be assigned. If an accused person thinks that the case against them is strong and that they will be copping out, it would be a good idea for them to see if their attorney can arrange for them to make a plea bargain. The reason why is because their case has not yet gone before the grand jury and the district attorney is in a better position to offer them a lower plea bargain than they would be if the suspect is indicted. If the case goes to the grand jury later and the accused is indicted, there are certain mandatory minimums depending on the nature of the crime and their criminal history that the prosecutor will have to abide by. Whereas, if they are about to be arraigned after their first court appearance, their lawyer can request a plea offer from the district attorney in order to dispose of the case at an early juncture. All criminal defendants have a right to the "effective assistance of counsel." This means that even a court appointed attorney must be vigilant in protecting a defendant's fundamental rights during all proceedings that are held regarding a particular case. See Strickland v. Washington, 466 U.S. 668, 104 S.Ct. 2052 (1984).

GRAND JURIES

GRAND JURY PROCEEDINGS

According to the Fifth Amendment of the United States Constitution "no person shall be held to answer for a capital, or otherwise infamous crime, unless on a presentment or indictment of a Grand Jury." The purpose of grand juries is to determine "whether there is probable cause to believe a crime has been committed and...[to protect]... citizens against unfounded criminal prosecutions." United States v. Calandra, 414 U.S. 338, 343, 94 S.Ct. 613, 617 (1974).

Grand jury proceedings are usually conducted in secrecy to protect witnesses of a crime and grand jurors. It also prevents the flight of a potential suspect who doesn't know that they are the subject of a grand jury investigation. Grand juries are comprised of a body of citizens who hear evidence presented regarding possible criminal activity and decide whether or not the evidence is "legally sufficient" to bring an accused party to trial. A grand jury must consist of a Quorum, or 16 to 23 people who have heard all of the evidence presented by the DA in a particular case. People v. Collier, 72 N.Y.2d 298, 532 N.Y.S.2d 718 (1988). 12 grand jurors can vote an indictment which is then called a true bill. They can vote not to indict which is called no true bill, or they can return the case to criminal court to be prosecuted as a misdemeanor charge if they feel that there is not enough evidence to warrant felony charges.

Although prosecutors have wide latitude in their ability to present evidence before grand juries, an individual suspected of committing a crime still retains their Sixth Amendment right to confront their accusers in certain circumstances. For instance, a prosecutor cannot read certified transcripts of a suspect's plea and sentence from a previous conviction into evidence before a grand jury if the defendant never had the prior opportunity to cross-examine the witness. People v. Haran, 22 Misc.3d 283, 865 N.Y.S.2d 877 (EssexCo.2008); Crawford v. Washington, 541 U.S. 36, 124 S.Ct. 1354.

In most cases where criminal defendants are represented by public defenders or 18-b lawyers they are almost always told that they should not testify before the grand jury because it can hurt them more than it can help them in the long run. In some cases this may be true. However, that may not necessarily be the case in all situations. There was a situation once where two guys were having a shoot-out on a Brooklyn street. Each guy was across the street from the other, firing away. People who lived on the block witnessed what took place and after the shooting was over each of the shooters went their own way with neither of them being injured during the fracas. When the police arrived on the scene and canvassed the area there was a jeep parked on the block that belonged to a local resident. The windows were rolled down a little and one of the officers decided to open the door and take a look inside.

While the officer was searching the vehicle someone who knew the owner of the jeep went to her apartment and notified her that there were police looking through her vehicle. When she got downstairs to inquire into what was going on, she informed the officer that the vehicle being searched was hers. The officer then placed her under arrest and it wasn't until she was brought to the precinct that the officer informed her that a large amount of narcotics was allegedly found inside of a brown paper bag in the passenger seat.

Fortunately for this woman some of the people on her block who witnessed the incident were willing to come forward and tell her family that they saw one of the shooters toss something inside of her vehicle as they were shooting at the other person across the street. Her family immediately hired an attorney who interviewed those witnesses and put in a timely request to have her and her witnesses testify before the grand jury. After hearing their testimony the grand jury voted no true bill. Had her and her witnesses not testified, the grand jury would have only heard evidence of what was found and under what circumstances it was found. That alone would have more than likely resulted in a true bill being voted against this woman once they determined that it was in fact found in her jeep.

Once a person is arrested, their lawyer is notified if the DA intends to present their case to a grand jury. In New York State, individuals accused of crimes have the right to testify before the grand jury weighing the criminal charges. However, the accused must serve a written request of their desire to testify before the grand jury to the District Attorney's office in the county where the charges are pending. The accused must also state an address where communications may be sent regarding these proceedings.

POSTCONVICTION REMEDIES

Prior to the enactment of Criminal Procedure Law (CPL) §440.10 and §440.20, the Court of Appeals in New York allowed individuals convicted of a crime to petition to the original trial court or nisi prius court through a writ of coram nobis to seek redress of issues that couldn't he reviewed on direct appeal.

Under CPL §440.10 a criminal defendant can collaterally attack the judgment rendered against them. This motion is usually used to address issues that are off the record, issues that are not properly preserved for appellate review, or claims that can be otherwise brought in a 440.10 motion. Denial of counsel and an illegal guilty plea are two of the most highly litigated claims brought by incarcerated individuals. A claim of newly discovered evidence can also be brought where the evidence would have been beneficial to the defense and the verdict would have been more favorable to the defense had the new evidence been received at trial. Part of the hurdle that must be overcome with a newly discovered evidence claim is that the defendant could not have produced the new evidence with due diligence. However, once a defendant becomes aware of a claim they must exercise due diligence in litigating it. This simply means that they must make a motion to pursue the claim as soon as possible once they find out about it.

In the Sample 440.10 Motion that follows, the issue raised deals with an individual being denied their constitutional right to confront witnesses against them due to the failure of their trial attorney to cross-examine the witness. Instead, the lawyer entered into a stipulation with the prosecutor and the trial proceeded without the testimony of the forensic analyst who is supposed to have tested the evidence seized and found it to be cocaine of a certain weight. On June 25, 2009 the United States Supreme Court decided the case of Melendez-Diaz v. Massachusetts, 129 S.Ct. 2527, and determined that the certificates of forensic analysts that were introduced at the trial were admitted in violation of due process because the analysts did not testify at the trial and give the defense the opportunity to confront these witnesses whose 'testimonial statements' were introduced in the form of affidavits. The defendant's arguments in the Sample Motion provided are based on six key components:

1. The defendant was deprived of his right to confront witnesses against him at trial in violation of the Sixth and Fourteenth Amendments of the United States Constitution, and Article I, §6 of the New York State Constitution.
2. Trial counsel's failure to cross-examine the forensic analyst who prepared laboratory results resulted in such prejudice to the defense that defendant's right to the effective assistance of counsel was violated.
3. Trial counsel's failure to contest the forensic testing could not have produced a just result.
4. Trial counsel's failure to cross-examine the forensic analyst in this case deprived him of his right to due process.
5. Defense counsel's entering into a stipulation with the prosecution resulted in a presumptively unfair and unreliable trial.
6. Defense counsel should be ordered to submit an affidavit responding to the allegations in this motion.

In the Sample 440.10 Motion, the last ground raised is that "defense counsel should be ordered to submit an affidavit responding to the allegations in this motion." The reason for this is that CPL §440.30 outlines the procedures for the court to utilize in determining whether to grant or deny a 440.10 or 440.20 motion. Subdivision 4(b) of 440.30 gives the reviewing court the option to deny the motion where the papers do not contain an affidavit substantiating all of the facts necessary to prove whatever the claims are. Subdivision 1 states that the motion papers "must contain" sworn allegations by the defendant or another person. Where the other person is the trial lawyer, not many of them are going to provide a criminal defendant with an affidavit to support a claim that their performance was ineffective. Therefore, before a motion is drafted with such a claim, a letter should be forwarded to the lawyer asking them why they did whatever the action is that is being complained about, or why they failed to do whatever is intended to be complained about. An affidavit of service should be prepared as well, and the letter should be sent "certified-mail, return-receipt requested." This way, copies of the letters and the affidavit of service can be attached with the receipt as part of the motion to show that it was in fact sent and received by the attorney. In order for a petitioner to show entitlement to a hearing they must submit an affidavit from the attorney or explain why they failed to provide one. Pro se 440.10 motions get shot down all of the time because jailhouse lawyers do not cover this important base. Once this base is covered it will increase the chance of a hearing being held even if the issues have to be litigated all the way to federal court. Federal courts are getting tired of having to rule on collateral attacks of convictions where they have little or no record to go on because a hearing wasn't held in the lower state court to create one. See People v. Morales, 58 N.Y.2d 1008, 1009, 461 N.Y.S.2d 1011, 1012 (1983).

The first ground in our Motion that follows is not argued under ineffective assistance of counsel because the Melendez-Diaz decision was handed down by the court after the conviction was obtained. Ineffective assistance of counsel claims are measured under the laws that existed at the time the alleged ineffective assistance occurred. Therefore, this issue had to be argued under the applicable retroactivity principles provided for that purpose. *Always remember to include your exhibits with any motion you submit to the court!*

The Sample Motion pursuant to 440.20 is premised on a defendant having received a concurrent sentence in a State court after a federal sentence was already imposed. After serving the majority of the state sentence the individual was transferred to the custody of the federal authorities and discovered that although the sentences were supposed to be concurrent, the Federal Bureau of Prisons refused to credit them with anything more than the 39 days that wasn't already credited to the state sentence.

There are countless individuals throughout the states that have been subjected to the feds refusal to credit them with concurrent time for time served in a state facility. Under 18 U.S.C. §3585(b), The Bureau of Prisons (BOP) can refuse to credit someone with time already credited to another sentence. However, they can issue the credit if they choose to. Anyone serving a state sentence that is supposed to run concurrent to a previously imposed federal sentence in the United States should make the necessary moves to be transferred to a federal institution to begin serving the federal sentence in order to prevent this from happening to them. The United States Supreme Court cases cited in this work are binding in every state. Therefore, all it takes is for someone to Shepardize them in order to find the controlling precedents in their state and utilize the controlling precedents from the particular state along with the United States Supreme Court precedents.

The Sample Letter addressed to the Federal Bureau of Prisons and the Sample Memorandum of Law made in support of a petition for habeas corpus pursuant to 28 U.S.C. §2241 can be utilized for those in federal custody going through this experience. There is really no other way to challenge this issue successfully other than to exhaust their remedies by appealing to the BOP and raising the issues there first. A §2241 motion can be made under the "clear error of law," and "manifest injustice" standard. *If you are from New York and want to petition the court under 440.10 dealing with this issue, always remember that it is necessary to put the State and County where the papers are being notarized instead of leaving "STATE OF NEW YORK)," "COUNTY OF _____)" blank under the caption headings to your affidavits of motion. This applies to all other motions as well and lets the court know the state and county you are swearing to the truth of your paperwork in. After the exhaustion of remedies this issue can also be brought by a federal prisoner in a 28 U.S.C. 2255 petition for habeas corpus as well. *Always remember that you have to be able to cope and deal with the loss of issues in a particular court.* Also, never give up and always take it to the next level. A lot of pro se litigants get frustrated and give up on themselves even when they have good issues. Don't let that be you.

WHERE TO FILE A 440 MOTION

A motion made pursuant to 440.10 or 440.20 must be filed in the court where the conviction was obtained.

WHEN TO FILE

Motions made under the 440 statute should be made as soon as possible after you become aware of the issue(s). In a case where you are in the process of obtaining information that pertains to more than one issue it is better to wait until you have everything you need to raise all of your issues at one time instead of filing successive petitions. If your motion is based on "newly discovered evidence," or a "retroactive change in the law," you should prepare the argument and exercise "due diligence" with the filing of your motion.

WHAT TO FILE

(1) Cover letter to the Court Clerk explaining exactly what papers you are forwarding to the court along with your letter.

(2) Notice of Motion, Affidavit In Support of Motion, Exhibits and Affidavit of Service. Your return date on your motion should be at least 13 days after the date you are mailing your motion papers to the court. However, if you are still attempting to obtain a letter from the attorney who represented the case you should make the return date at least 30 days from the date of your motion and explain this to the court like we have done in the Sample 440.10 motion. There is no need to file a separate motion to request assignment of counsel or poor person's status because the requests are included in the actual motions themselves. However, if the court requests them you must submit them. If you are granted a hearing and the court determines that you are indigent they usually appoint counsel to represent such defendants at the hearing. In the event that your motion is denied you have to file an appeal within 30 days to the appellate division in whatever department has jurisdiction over the county where you filed your 440 motion. The appropriate appeal forms can be found in McKinney's Forms Books under CPL §460.15.

WHERE TO FILE

The original motion papers and a copy of your exhibits should be filed with the court in which you were convicted along with the original Affidavit of Service. A copy of the motion and affidavits should be sent to the county attorney and the district attorney in the same county. If you are filing in New York City (Manhattan) you have to send the papers to the office of Corporation Counsel instead of county attorney. Corporation Counsel, 100 Church Street, 4th Floor, New York, NY 10007.

WHAT TO EXPECT AFTER YOU FILE

Once you have filed your motion with the court and served copies upon the district attorney, county attorney and/or corporation counsel, the court clerk will process your papers and assign a judge to your case. 440 motions are usually always heard by the judge who handled the case unless they are retired or there is a conflict within the case where the judge is recused. The justice handling the case will require the prosecution to respond by a certain date and afterwards make a decision whether or not to grant a hearing, grant the motion, or deny the motion without a hearing. If the motion is denied it should always be appealed to the next level. The system designed the appeals process because they know the lower courts don't always make perfect decisions based on the law. If your issue has merit and you are consistent there is always the possibility that you will prevail.

SUPREME COURT OF THE STATE OF NEW YORK
COUNTY OF KINGS : PART K9
_____

THE PEOPLE OF THE STATE OF NEW YORK
        Respondent,
        -AGAINST-
_____, #_____
        Defendant.
_____

****
(SAMPLE)
MOTION TO VACATE JUDGEMENT
KINGS COUNTY INDICTMENT NUMBER 14326-07
****

Petitioner Pro Se
Attica Corr. Facility
P.O. Box 149
Attica, N.Y. 14011

CONTENTS

Table Of Authorities 29
Notice Of Motion To Vacate Judgement 33
Affidavit In Support Of Motion To Vacate Judgement 36
Procedural History 37
Facts 38
    Mapp/Dunaway Hearing 38
    The Trial 39
    Stipulation 40
    Robert Chance 41
    Summation 42
    The Verdict 43
    The Sentence 43
    The Appeal 43
Ground I 44
    Defendant Was Deprived Of His Right To Confront Witnesses Against Him At Trial In Violation Of The Sixth And Fourteenth Amendments Of The U.S. Constitution, And Article I, §6 Of The New York State Constitution. 44

Ground II...58

    Trial Counsel's Failure To Cross-Examine The Forensic Analyst Who Prepared Laboratory Reports Resulted In Such Prejudice To The Defense That Defendant's Right To The Effective Assistance Of Counsel Was Violated (U.s. Const. Amends. VI And XIV; N.Y. Const., Art. I, §6)..58

    A. Trial Counsel's Failure To Contest The Forensic Testing Could Not Have Produced A Just Result.........61

    B. Trial Counsel's Failure To Cross-Examine The Forensic Analyst In This Case Deprived Him Of His Right To Due Process. 63

    C. Defense Counsel's Stipulation Entered Into With The Prosecution Resulted In A Presumtpively Unfair And Unreliable Trial. 65

Ground III 67

    Defense Trial Counsel Should Be Ordered To Submit An Affidavit Responding To The Allegations In This Motion. 67

Conclusion.. 91

TABLE OF AUTHORITIES

<u>CASES</u>

Chambers v. Mississippi, 410 U.S. 284 (1973) 54
Chapman v. California, 386 U.S. 18 (1967) 55
Crawford v. Washington, 541 U.S. 36 (2004) 44
Cruz v. New York, 481 U.S. 186 (1987) 53
Danforth v. Minnesota, ___ U.S. ___ (2004) 54
Davis v. Washington, 547 U.S. 813 (2006) 63
Delaware v. Van Arsdall, 475 U.S. 673 (1986) 56
Dowdell v. United States, 221 U.S. 325 (1911) 64
Kirby v. United States, 174 U.S. 47 (1899) 50
Mattox v. United States, 156 U.S. 237 (1895) 64
Melendez-Diaz v. Massachusetts, 551 U.S. ___ (2009) 47
Murray v. Carrier, 477 U.S. 478 (1986) 68
Ohio v. Roberts, 448 U.S. 56 (1980) 50
Olden v. Kentucky, 488 U.S. 227 (1988) 52
People v. Baldi, 54 N.Y.2d 137 (1981) 59
People v. Benevento, 91 N.Y.2d 137 (1998) 59
People v. Brown, 28 N.Y.2d 282 (1971) 68
People v. Eastman, 85 N.Y.2d 265 (1995) 52
People v. Guidice, 83 N.Y. 2d 630 (1994) 46

People v. Henry, 95 N.Y.2d 563 (2000) 59
People v. Klaus, 94 A.D.2d 748 (2d Dept.1983) 66
People v. Morales, 58 N.Y.2d 1008 (1983) 68
People v. Pacer, 6 N.Y.3d 504 (2006) 46
People v. Satterfield., 66 N.Y.2d 796 (1985) 60
People v. Scott, 10 N.Y.2d 380 (1961) 69
People v. Stultz, 2 N.Y.3d 277 (2004) 61
People v. Sullivan, 56 N.Y.2d 378 (1982) 51
Pointer v. Texas, 380 U.S. 400 (1965) 44
PPX Enterprises, Inc., v. Audiofidelity,
Inc., 746 F.2d 66 (2dCir.1984) 66
Sinicropi v. Milone, 915 F.2d 66 (2dCir.1990) 66
Strickland v. Washington, 466 U.S. 668 (1984) 60
Teague v. Lane, 489 U.S. 288 (1989) 54
United States v. Towne, 870 F.2d 880 (2dCir.1989) 56

STATUTES

Federal Rules of Evidence §803(6)(8) 46
N.Y. Civil Rights Law, Art. II, §12 45
N.Y. County Law §722 78
N.Y. CPL §440.10 33
N.Y. CPL §440.30 34
N.Y. CPLR §1101 37
N.Y. CPLR.§1102 37
N.Y. CPLR §4518(a) 46
N.Y. Judiciary Law §2-b 37
N.Y. Penal Law §210.45 51
N.Y. Penal Law §220.18 38

CONSTITUTIONAL PROVISIONS
N.Y. Const., Art. I, §6 34
U.S. Const., Amend. 6 36
U.S. Const., Amend. 14 36

REFERENCE MATERIALS
Black's Law Dictionary 62 (8th ed.2004) 47
16 C.J.S. §2113 (1918) 51
Paul C. Gianelli, The Admissibility of Laboratory
Reports in Criminal Trials The Reliability of
Scientific Proof, 49 Ohio St.L.J. 671 62
2 P. Gianelli & E. Imwinkelried, Scientific
Evidence, §23.03[c] (4th ed.2007) 57
Project Advisory Committee, Laboratory
Proficiency Testing. Program, Supplementary
Report-Samples 6-10, (1976) 62
Metzger, Cheating the Constitution,
59 Vand.L.Rev. 475 (2006) 62
United States Dep't of Justice Drug Enforcement
Administration & Executive Office of the President,
Office of National Drug Control Policy, Counterdrug
Technology Assessment Center, Scientific Working
Group for the Analysis of Seized Drugs (SWGDRUG)
Recommendations, at 14-16 (3d ed.2007-08-09) 61
Yael V. Levy, Federal Review of Procedural Bars to
Ineffective Assistance Claims, N.Y.L.J.,
pp. 4, 8(October 5, 2009) 68

SUPREME COURT OF THE STATE OF NEW YORK
COUNTY OF KINGS
---------------------------------------X

The People of the State of New York

       Plaintiffs,   (SAMPLE)
                          NOTICE OF MOTION TO
       -against-   VACATE JUDGEMENT

_____,
Defendant.   IND. NO._____

---------------------------------------X

    PLEASE TAKE NOTICE, that upon the annexed affidavit of
_____, sworn to on the _____ day of _____, 20_____, and all the documents attached thereto, and upon the accusatory instrument and all of the proceedings had herein, the petitioner will move this Court at Part _____ thereof, at the Courthouse located at 320 Jay Street, Brooklyn, NY 11201 on the _____ day of _____, 20_____ at 9:30 a.m., or as soon thereafter as counsel may be heard for:

    (1) an Order pursuant to Criminal Procedure Law §440.10(1)(h), vacating the judgment heretofore entered upon the above-named defendant on the 6th day of February, 2010 or, in the alternative, ordering a

hearing to determine whether such judgment should be vacated on the grounds that:

(A) DEFENDANT WAS DEPRIVED OF HIS RIGHT TO CONFRONT WITNESSES AGAINST HIM AT TRIAL IN VIOLATION OF THE SIXTH AND FOURTEENTH AMENDMENTS OF THE U.S. CONSTITUTION, AND ARTICLE I, §6 OF THE NEW YORK STATE CONSTITUTION.

(B) TRIAL COUNSEL'S FAILURE TO CROSS-EXAMINE THE FORENSIC ANALYST WHO PREPARED LABORATORY REPORTS RESULTED IN SUCH PREJUDICE TO THE DEFENSE THAT DEFENDANT'S RIGHT TO THE EFFECTIVE ASSISTANCE OF COUNSEL WAS VIOLATED UNDER U.S. CONST. AMENDS. VI AND XIV; N.Y. CONST., ART. I, §6.

(2) Defendant is currently confined at _____

_____

and it is requested that the Court, pursuant to New York Criminal Procedure Law §440.30(5), cause the defendant who is confined as hereinabove stated, to be produced at any hearing which the Court shall conduct to determine this motion; and

(3) Such other and further relief as to the Court may seem just and proper.

PLEASE TAKE FURTHER NOTICE, that pursuant to C.P.L.R. §2214(b), answering affidavits, if any, are required to be served upon the undersigned at least seven (7) days before the return date of this motion.

Dated: _____, ___, 20__.
         _____, New York

TO:_____   _____
District Attorney   Defendant Pro Se
Kings County   _____
Brooklyn, New York   _____
                          _____

SUPREME COURT OF THE STATE OF NEW YORK
COUNTY OF KINGS
---------------------------------------X
The People of the State of New York

    Plaintiffs,   (SAMPLE)
           AFFIDAVIT IN SUPPORT
  -against-   **OF MOTION TO VACATE**
           JUDGEMENT

  Defendant.
         IND. NO._____
---------------------------------------X
STATE OF NEW YORK)
)ss.:
COUNTY OF _____)

  _____, being duly sworn deposes and says:

  1. I am the defendant herein and I am currently incarcerated at _____.

  2. I make this affidavit in support of my motion pursuant to CPL §440.10(1)(h) of the New York Criminal Procedure Law for an Order vacating the judgment of conviction in the above entitled matter on the ground(s) that:

  (1) I was deprived of my right to confront witnesses against me at trial in violation of the Sixth and Fourteenth Amendments of the U.S. Constitution, and Article I, §6 of the New York State Constitution; and

  (2) I was denied the effective assistance of counsel at trial in violation of the Sixth and Fourteenth Amendments of the U.S.

Constitution, and Article I, §6 of the New York State Constitution.

3. This affidavit is also made in support of my requests (a) for an Order pursuant to Judiciary Law §2—b[3], directing attorney Mr. Brian Rogers, Esq., to serve and file an affidavit responding to the allegations made hereinafter about his trial performance on the ground that such a responding affidavit is necessary to carry into effect the powers and jurisdiction possessed by the Court, and to better serve the interests of judicial time and economy; (b) for an Order, pursuant to C.P.L.R. §1101 and 1102, assigning an attorney to represent me in this proceeding on the ground that I cannot afford such professional services needed to argue the merits of my issues for a proper determination of my motion to vacate judgment; (c) for an Order, pursuant to C.P.L. §440.30(5), granting an evidentiary hearing on the ground that one is essential to create the evidentiary record necessary for the Court to adequately, effectively and meaningfully determine my motion to vacate judgment; and (d) for an Order, granting defendant's motion to vacate judgment; and (e) for an Order granting such other and further relief as to the Court may seem just and proper.

PROCEDURAL HISTORY

4. I was indicted by a Kings County grand jury charging defendant with criminal possession of a controlled substance in the

second degree, and convicted before Hon. Ranghelle, Judge, after a jury trial in which I didn't testify. I was represented by attorney Brian Rogers, Esq. Said conviction was for one count of the crime of criminal possession of a controlled substance 2°, in violation of penal law §220.18, Exhibit "A" annexed.

5. I was sentenced on May 22nd, 2009 to a determinate term of 10 years with 5 years postrelease supervision as a result of said judgment.

6. Due to the failure of my trial attorney to file a timely notice of appeal, I filed a motion for extension of time for taking an appeal in the Appellate Division for the Second Department. Said motion is still pending. Exhibits "B" and "C" annexed.

7. No previous application for the relief sought herein has been made to this or any other Court.

FACTS
MAPP/DUNAWAY HEARING

8. On December 10, 2008 a Mapp/Dunaway hearing was held in the instant matter. At the hearing Police Officer Freeman testified as to his version of the facts and circumstances surrounding defendant's arrest on November 8, 2007. After direct examination by the prosecution, and cross-examination by defense counsel the Court reserved its decision. In a Decision and Order dated January 30, 2009 the Court concluded that

probable cause existed for defendant's arrest and denied his motion to suppress the evidence. See Exhibits "D" and "E".

THE TRIAL

9. On November 8, 2007, Officer Freeman was assigned to the Anti-Crime Unit of the 79th Precinct and was working a 6:00 p.m. to 2:00 a.m. tour of duty. Freeman was in plain clothes and riding in an unmarked police vehicle with Police Officer Mobley, who was the driver. See T.T.5. [all references indicated as 'T.T.' are the appropriate pages of the Trial Transcript annexed hereto as Exhibit "D"].

10. According to Freeman, at approximately 11:18 p.m., they were in the vicinity of Lafayette Avenue and Franklin Avenue near the Lafayette Gardens Housing Complex when he observed a vehicle parked in the "no standing zone." Freeman then stated that as they approached the vehicle he observed an individual attempt to enter the vehicle, but that she fled and the individual in the driver's seat sped off in the car, drove on the sidewalk, and made a right turn on Franklin Avenue. T.T.6-8.

11. The fleeing vehicle struck another vehicle which was crossing the intersection at Franklin Avenue and Clifton Place. The driver then exited the vehicle and fled. Freeman then chased and apprehended the defendant on Clifton Place. As Freeman chased the defendant he observed him take

a bag from his waistband and toss it into a pile of garbage bags. After arresting the defendant he returned to recover the item that had been thrown away and found a large white ziplock bag inside of which was another sandwich-like bag tied in a knot containing a white substance and tubular type packaging. He then took these items to the property clerk at the precinct where it received Voucher Number B123456, and then was forwarded to the police laboratory for analysis. T.T.8-18.

12. Sgt. Waters testified that he was the Supervising Officer of the Anti-Crime unit on November 8, 2007. After arriving to the scene of defendant's arrest, Officer Freeman and Officer Mobley informed him that they had arrested defendant once they found him to be in possession of a white rocky substance.

Stipulation

13. Unknown to the defendant was the fact that the prosecutor and defense counsel entered into a stipulation concerning what the forensic analyst would testify to if he were called to testify at the trial. Also unknown to the defendant was the fact that defense counsel waived his right to confront the analyst after he told defendant that the analyst would be called to testify at the trial. Rather than have the analyst testify, defense counsel chose to allow the stipulation to enter into the trial containing erroneous information that would

have amounted to the analyst perjuring himself if he testified to the contents of the stipulation's accuracy.

Robert Chance

14. The stipulation signed by the defense counsel and the prosecutor states that Robert Chance, if called to testify, would have testified that he is a chemist employed by NYPD's laboratory. That he received a degree in chemical engineering from University of Calicut, and has served as a chemist at the NYPD laboratory since April of 2000. That Mr. Chance has performed in excess of 6,000 tests to determine the presence or absence of heroin or cocaine, and that the Court would have declared and accepted his testimony as that of an expert witness.

15. The stipulation further states that Mr. Chance would have testified that he "received the People's exhibit 2 on **November 25, 2007,** sealed from the evidence clerk at the lab." He then performed a series of tests on the powder to determine whether heroin or cocaine were present. Based upon the results of these tests, Mr. Chance determined to a reasonable degree of scientific certainty that the substance contained the narcotic drug cocaine, and that it weighed in excess of four ounces. Exhibit "G" annexed.

16. The Controlled Substance Analysis Worksheet endorsed by Mr. Chance indicates that on **November 23, 2007,** Mr. Chance was in possession of Voucher No. B123456, and had

begun running tests on Item #3, Item # 1, and Item #2. It further indicates that on **November 24, 2007,** testing was continued on Item #2, and that Mr. Chance then proceeded to test Items #2A and #2B. It also notes that Mr. Chance tested the material using one testing method. See Exhibit "F".

17. Upon closer examination of these documents it becomes clear that Mr. Chance would have been guilty of perjuring himself for testifying that "he received the contents of the prosecutor's exhibit **#2** on **November 25, 2007** sealed from the evidence clerk at the lab" when his lab reports indicate that the testing actually began two days before on **November 23, 2007,** and resumed on **November 24, 2007.** This is further evidenced by the substance analysis report sworn to by Mr. Chance attesting to the fact that Mr. Chance received these materials on **November 20, 2007.** Defense counsel, however, allowed this erroneous information in the stipulation to be utilized at the trial along with Mr. Chance's forensic analysis reports without assessing it's inaccuracies, or exerting defendant's constitutional right to cross-examine Mr. Chance. Cf. Exhibits "F" and "G".

Summation

18. During the prosecutor's summation, the assistant district attorney held up the erroneous stipulation and the lab reports and told the jurors that "this is what they would have testified to if they were called to

testify." Notwithstanding the fact that the stipulation contains conflicting information, defense counsel allowed this information to enter into defendant's trial without making sure that the information was accurate. Defense counsel also waived defendant's right to confront the analyst and failed to render a timely objection.[1]

The Verdict

19. On May 4, 2009 the jury found defendant guilty of one count of criminal possession of a controlled substance in the second degree. T.T.460.

The Sentence

20. On May 22, 2009 the defendant was sentenced to a 10 year determinate sentence with 5 years postrelease supervision.

The Appeal

21. After the sentencing proceedings, it is based upon information and belief that defense counsel failed to file a timely Notice of Appeal on defendant's behalf. As a result of this, defendant has filed a Motion for Extension of Time For Taking Appeal. Said motion is currently pending before the Appellate Division, Second Department.

---

[1] Prior to the trial in this matter, the Appellate Division for the Second Department had already held that accusations founded on erroneous stipulations cannot stand. See People v. Klaus, 94 A.D.2d 748, 462 N.Y.S.2d 498 (1983).

22. In a letter dated December 5, 2009 defendant asked defense trial counsel why he failed to require that the lab analyst testify, and why did he waive defendant's right to confront the forensic analyst. Defendant also inquired as to why defense counsel failed to file an appeal on his behalf. To date defense counsel has not responded. Exhibits "B" "H" and "I". This proceeding ensued.

ARGUMENT

GROUND I

DEFENDANT WAS DEPRIVED OF HIS RIGHT TO CONFRONT WITNESSES AGAINST HIM AT TRIAL IN VIOLATION OF THE SIXTH AND FOURTEENTH AMENDMENTS OF THE U.S. CONSTITUTION, AND ARTICLE I, §6 OF THE NEW YORK STATE CONSTITUTION.

The Sixth Amendment to the United States Constitution, made applicable to the States via the Fourteenth Amendment, Pointer v. Texas, 380 U.S. 400, 403 (1965), provides that "[i]n all criminal prosecutions, the accused shall enjoy the right...to be confronted with the witnesses against him." In Crawford v. Washington, 541 U.S. 36, after reviewing the Clause's historical underpinnings, the Supreme Court held that it guarantees a defendant's right to confront those "who bear testimony," against him. A witness's testimony against a defendant is thus inadmissible unless the witness appears at trial, or if the witness is unavailable, the defendant had a prior opportunity for cross-examination. Crawford v. Washington, 541 U.S. 36, 51, 54; See Also N.Y. Const., Article I, §6; N.Y. Civil Rights Law, Bill of Rights, Article 2, §12.

In Crawford, the Court held that "testimonial" statements not previously subjected to cross-examination are inadmissible against a criminal defendant. The Court did not fully spell out what is "testimonial," but offered some guidance. It referred to "[various formulations" of the "core class of 'testimonial' statements," including:

> "'ex parte in-court testimony or its functional equivalent that is, material such as affidavits, custodial examinations, prior testimony that the defendant was unable to cross-examine, or similar pretrial statements that declarants would reasonably expect to be used prosecutorially,' ... 'extrajudicial statements... contained in formalized testimonial materials, such as affidavits, depositions, prior testimony, or confessions,' [and] 'statements that were made under circumstances which would lead an objective witness reasonably to believe that the statement would be

available for use at a later trial.'" Crawford v. Washington, 541 U.S. at 51-52, 124 S.Ct. 1353 [citations omitted].

Although Crawford repeatedly describes affidavits as typically being testimonial, not all affidavits are inadmissible. The Crawford Court concluded that business records would not have been considered testimonial at the time the Confrontation Clause was adopted. People v. Pacer, 6 N.Y.3d 504, 510.

Under New York rules of evidence, unlike the federal rules included within Federal Rules of Evidence, rule 803[6][8], "law enforcement agencies constitute businesses for the purpose of the rule." People v. Guidice, 83 N.Y.2d 630, 635, 612 N.Y.S.2d 350 [1994].

C.P.L.R. §4518(a), New York's business records exception to the hearsay prohibition provides:

> "Any writing or record, whether in the form of an entry in a book or otherwise, made as a memorandum or record of any act, transaction, occurrence or event, shall be admissible in evidence of proof of that act, transaction, occurrence or event, if the judge finds that it was made in the regular course of any such business to make it at the time of the act, transaction, occurrence

or event, or within a reasonable time thereafter."

In the instant matter, the Police Department's analyst's laboratory reports prepared for use in the defendant's criminal trial fall within the "core class of testimonial statements" outlined in Crawford. "[T]he Confrontation Clause is implicated by extrajudicial statements only insofar as they are contained in formalized testimonial materials, such as affidavits, depositions, prior testimony, or confessions." The documents at issue here, while denominated by New York law "certificates," are quite plainly affidavits, i.e., "declaration[s] of facts written down and sworn to by the declarant before an officer authorized to administer oaths." Black's Law Dictionary, 62, (8th ed.2004). They are incontrovertibly a "'solemn declaration or affirmation made for the purpose of establishing or proving some fact.'" Crawford v. Washington, 541 U.S. at 51, quoting, 2 N. Webster, An American Dictionary of the English Language (1828).

In the recently decided case of Melendez-Diaz v. Massachusetts, 551 U.S. _____, 129 S.Ct. 2527 (2009), decided on June 25, 2009, the prosecutor introduced certificates of state laboratory analysts at the petitioner's state-court drug trial stating that the material seized by police and connected to petitioner was cocaine of a certain quantity. As required by Massachusetts law, the certificates were sworn to before a notary public and were admitted as prima facie evidence of what they asserted. Petitioner objected asserting that Crawford v. Washington, 541 U.S. 36, required the analysts to testify in person. The trial court disagreed, the certificates were admitted, and petitioner was convicted. The Massachusetts appeals court affirmed, rejecting petitioner's claim that the certificates' admission violated the Sixth Amendment. In determining whether the introduction of these certificates violated the defendant's right to confrontation, the United States Supreme court held that:

> (a) Under Crawford, a witness's testimony against a defendant is inadmissible unless the witness appears at trial or, if the witness is unavailable, the defendant had a prior opportunity for cross-examination. 541 U.S. at 54. The certificates here are affidavits, which fall within the "core class of testimonial statements" covered by the Confrontation Clause, id., at 51. They asserted that the substance found in petitioner's possession was, as the prosecution claimed, cocaine of a certain weight - the precise testimony the analysts would be expected to provide if called at trial. Not only were the certificates made, as Crawford

required for testimonial statements, "under circumstances which would lead an objective witness reasonably to believe that the statement would be available for use at a later trial," id., at 52, but under relevant Massachusetts law their sole purpose was to provide prima facie evidence of the substance's composition, quality, and net weight. Petitioner was entitled to "be confronted with" the persons giving this testimony at trial. id., at 54.

(b) The arguments advanced to avoid this rather straightforward application of Crawford are rejected. Respondents claim that the analysts are not subject to confrontation because they are not "accusatory" witnesses finds no support in the Sixth Amendment's texts or in this Court's case law. The affiants' testimonial statements were not "nearly contemporaneous" with their observations, nor, if they had been, would that fact alter the statements' testimonial character. There is no support for the proposition that witnesses who testify regarding facts other than those observed at the crime scene are exempt from confrontation. The absence of interrogation is irrelevant; a witness who volunteers his testimony is no less a witness for Sixth Amendment purposes, the affidavits do not qualify as traditional official or business records. The argument that the analysts should not be subject to confrontation because their statements results from neutral scientific testing is little more than an invitation to return to the since-overruled decision in Ohio v. Roberts, 448 U.S. 56, 66, which held that evidence with "particularized guarantees of trustworthiness" was admissible without confrontation. Melendez-Diaz v. Massachusetts, 557 U.S., 129 S.Ct. 2527, at 2529 (2009).

The confrontation violation that occurs when, as here, forensic laboratory reports are introduced to establish an element of the crime at issue is particularly acute. In Kirby v. United States, 174 U.S. 47 (1899), the prosecution introduced a record of a co-conspirator's guilty plea for larceny to prove that property that the defendant had received was stolen. The Supreme Court held that the introducing of this record violated the Confrontation Clause because it served to prove, by means of unconfronted testimony, a "vital fact which the government was bound to establish affirmatively." Id., at 55-56. In other words, the introduction of the co-conspirator's statement of guilt, which the defendant was unable to cross-examine, unconstitutionally "enable[d] the government to put the accused, although shielded by the presumption of innocence, upon the defensive" concerning an element of the charge. Id., at 60-61. A contemporaneous treatise elaborated upon this holding:

> "[R]ecords are not admissible to prove the acts constituting the offense itself. Where a document or record relates to facts which are not such as can be proved only by an original or a certified copy, but may be established by oral testimony...the constitutional guaranty [of confrontation] applies." 16 C.J.S. §2113, at 837-838 (1918).

Such is precisely the case here. One of the elements of the crime with which petitioner was charged was that he possessed cocaine of a certain weight. In order to establish these elements, the prosecution offered the forensic analyst's sworn certificate and laboratory reports.[2] And the jury was instructed that it could find the defendant possessed cocaine based on this evidence alone. To the extent that the analyst was a witness, he certainly provided testimony against the defendant, proving one fact necessary for his conviction, that

---

[2] The certificate here was attested to under N.Y. Penal Law §210.45 which was enacted by legislature to "provide a convenient method of assuring truthfulness of documents without requiring an oath before a notary." See People v. Sullivan, 56 N.Y.2d 378, 452 N.Y.S.2d 373 (1982).

the substance he possessed was cocaine of a certain weight. While the confrontation clause guarantees a defendant the right to be confronted with the witnesses "against him," the Compulsory Process Clause guarantees a defendant the right to call witnesses "in his favor." The text of the Amendment contemplates two classes of witnesses, those against the defendant and those in his favor. The prosecution must produce the former; the defendant may call the latter. As the Court held in Melendez-Diaz, "there is not a third category of witnesses, helpful to the prosecution, but somehow immune from confrontation." Melendez-Diaz, 557 U.S., 129 S.Ct. 2527, 2534.

In short, the lack of a live witness for the defense to confront "eliminated defendant's opportunity to contest a 'decisive piece' of evidence against him." This is exactly the evil the Confrontation Clause was designed to prevent. People v. Pacer, 6 N.Y.3d 504, 512 (2006), 814 N.Y.S.2d 575.

Retroactivity

After determining that the forensic analyst's sworn certificate is a testimonial statement within the meaning of Melendez-Diaz, the court must then turn on the question of whether the admission of these testimonial statements require defendant's conviction to be set aside on collateral review. As set forth by the Court of Appeals in People v. Eastman, 85 N.Y. 2d 265, 624

N.Y.S.2d 83, determining whether a conviction should be set aside on collateral review requires a two-step analysis. The first step involves a determination as to whether the introduction of the forensic analyst's testimonial statements was harmless error. The Court of Appeals, in Eastman considered the question of a defendant's collateral attack on his conviction based on an alleged violation of the Sixth Amendment's Confrontation Clause, as delineated by a new rule issued by the United States Supreme Court. Specifically, the Court of Appeals determined that Cruz v. New York, 481 U.S. 186, which held that the confrontation Clause bars the introduction of a non-testifying co-defendant's confession that implicates the defendant, applied retroactively to the defendant's collateral attack on his conviction. In doing so, the Court of Appeals set forth the test for determining whether a new United States Supreme Court rule applies retroactively on collateral review.

Eastman held that when a Supreme Court holding "marks a break from both Federal and State law precedent" and "fundamentally alters the Federal constitutional landscape, the principles of retroactivity developed by the Supreme Court in construing Federal constitutional law govern the disposition of the case." People v. Eastman, 85 N.Y.2d 265, 275, 624 N.Y.S.2d 83.

In the case of Danforth v. Minnesota, the Supreme Court held that: "no federal rule, either implicitly announced in Teague, or in some other source of federal law, prohibits States from giving broader retroactive effect to new rules of criminal procedure. Danforth v. Minnesota, _____ U.S. _____, 128 S.Ct. 1029, 1046-1047; Cf. Teague v. Lane, 489 U.S. 288, 109 S.Ct. 1060 (1989).

The Court in Danforth reasoned that, "our opinion in Crawford announced a 'new rule' -- as that term is defined in Teague -- because the result in that case was not dictated by precedent existing at the time the defendant's conviction became final." Here, the defendant's case is not final, and the Melendez-Diaz rule falls within the "new rule" exception since it developed the definition of "testimonial evidence" that the Crawford Court left "for another day," and it involves the same "bedrock procedural element which implicates the fundamental fairness and accuracy of the trial," as in Cruz, i.e., the right to confrontation; "one of the fundamental guarantees of life and liberty." Kirby v. United States, 174 U.S. 47, 55, 19 S.Ct. 574 (1899); See Also Chambers v. Mississippi, 410 U.S. 284, 295, 93 S.Ct. 1038 (1973) ("The right to confrontation is more than a constitutional right of confrontation"); Pointer v. Texas, 380 U.S. 400, 405, 85 S.Ct. 1065 (1965) ("The right of cross-examination is an essential and fundamental requirement for the kind of fair trial which is the country's constitutional goal"). For the above reasons, the Melendez-Diaz rule must be applied retroactively on collateral review to the non-testifying forensic analyst's testimonial statements.

Using the aforementioned rationale, this court should conclude that the Melendez-Diaz rule applies retroactively, and follow that the non-testifying witnesses testimonial statements received in evidence against the defendant was in error since the non-testifying witnesses statements were admitted without affording the defendant the opportunity to cross-examine and test the reliability of those statements. Danforth v. Minnesota, ____ U.S. ____, 128 S.Ct. 1029, 1046 ("the absence of any precedent for the claim that Teague limits state collateral review courts' authority to provide remedies for federal constitutional violations is a sufficient reason for concluding that there is no such rule of federal law").

Harmless Error Analysis

The retroactivity of the Melendez-Diaz rule on collateral review alone is insufficient to require setting aside the defendant's conviction. Eastman reminds us that "the proper standard for review of Confrontation clause errors is harmless error analysis." People v. Eastman, 85 N.Y.2d 265, 276, 614 N.Y.S.2d 83; See Also Chapman v. California, 386 U.S. 18, 87 S.Ct. 824 (1967).

A harmless error analysis depends on consideration of such factors as "the importance of the testimony in the prosecution's case, whether the testimony was cumulative, the presence or absence of evidence corroborating or contradicting the testimony of the witness on material points, the extent of cross-examination otherwise permitted, and of course, the overall strength of the prosecutor's case." See Delaware v. Van Arsdall, 475 U.S. 673 at 684, 106 S.Ct. 1431; See Also Olden v. Kentucky, 488 U.S. 227, 109 S.Ct. 480 (1988); United States v. Towne, 870 F.2d 880, 886-887 (2d Cir.1989).

In looking at the entire record and the violations' "probable impact on the minds of an average jury," People v. Eastman, 85 N.Y.2d 265, 276, it would seem that the instant motion must be granted. The introduction of the forensic analyst's statements cannot be said to have been harmless error beyond a reasonable doubt. The evidence properly admitted in this case was insufficient to sustain the prosecutor's burden of proving beyond a reasonable doubt that the material allegedly seized by the police from the defendant was cocaine of a certain quantity required by CPL §220.18. The circumstances surrounding defendant's arrest and possession of the materials in question was established through the testimony of police officers Freeman, Mobley, and Sgt. Waters. However, the record is devoid of any information pertaining to what tests the analyst performed, whether those tests were routine, and whether interpreting the results required the exercise of judgment or the use of skills that the analyst may not have possessed. See 2 P. Gianelli & E. Imwinkelried, Scientific Evidence, §23.03[c], pp. 532-533, ch. 23A, p. 607 (4th ed.2007) (identifying four "critical errors" that analysts may commit in interpreting the results of the commonly used gas chromatography/mass spectrometry analysis); See Also Metzger, Cheating the Constitution, 59 Vand.L.Rev. 475, 491 (2006) ("[t]he legal community now conceded, with varying degrees of urgency, that our system produces erroneous convictions based on discredited forensics").

The nature of the impact of the forensic analyst's certification and lab reports on the mind of the average juror was extreme prejudice to the defendant, eliminating any possibility that the jury would accept the defense theory that the defendant wasn't involved in any criminal activity on November 8, 2007. It is the analyst's "testimonial" statements that supports defendant's conviction because only the analyst's statements attest that the analyst tested the substance and found it to be cocaine in excess of four ounces. Neither of the officers statements at trial do anything other than place defendant at the crime scene where he is said to have been found in possession of a "white rocky substance." Their statements do not explain the circumstances under which the material was tested and weighed. It is the "testimonial" nature of the forensic analyst's statements that provides the needed support for the defendant's conviction. This court should therefore conclude that the defendant's conviction could only have resulted because his Sixth Amendment right to confrontation was abridged by the admission of the analyst's "testimonial statements." As this error was harmful, defendant is entitled to a new trial. See Crawford v. Washington, 541 U.S. 36, at 61-62 (Dispensing with confrontation because testimony is obviously reliable is akin to dispensing with jury trial because defendant is obviously guilty. This is not what the Sixth Amendment prescribes").

Accordingly, defendant's CPL §440.10 motion should be granted, defendant's conviction of criminal possession in the second degree vacated, and a new trial ordered.

GROUND II

TRIAL COUNSEL'S FAILURE TO CROSS-EXAMINE THE FORENSIC ANALYST WHO PREPARED LABORATORY REPORTS RESULTED IN SUCH PREJUDICE TO THE DEFENSE THAT DEFENDANT'S RIGHT TO THE EFFECTIVE ASSISTANCE OF COUNSEL WAS VIOLATED (U.S. CONST. AMENDS. VI AND XIV; N.Y. CONST., ART. I, §6).

Defendant was denied the effective assistance of counsel in violation of his State and Federal constitutional rights due to trial counsel's failure to protect defendant's constitutional right to be confronted with the witnesses against him, and by defense counsel entering into an erroneous stipulation with the prosecution regarding a witness against him. Trial counsel failed in his duty to subject the prosecution's case to meaningful adversarial testing and resulted in a presumptively unfair and unreliable trial. Defense counsel's representation was "less than meaningful," and there is a "reasonable probability that but for counsels' unprofessional errors, the result of the proceedings would have been different." People v. Baldi, 54 N.Y.2d 137, 444 N.Y.S.2d 893 (1981); People v. Benevento, 91 N.Y.2d 708, 674 N.Y.S.2d 629; Strickland v. Washington, 466 U.S. 668, 104 S.Ct. 2052.

The right to effective assistance of counsel in criminal proceedings is guaranteed by the New York and Federal Constitutions. Our state standard for effective assistance of counsel "has long been whether the defendant was afforded 'meaningful representation.'" See U.S. Const., 6th Amend.; N.Y. Const., Art. I, §6; See Also People v. Henry, 95 N.Y.2d 563 (2000), quoting People v. Benevento, 91 N.Y.2d 708, 712, 674 N.Y.S.2d 628 (1998).

In applying this standard, the Court of Appeals has emphasized the difference between ineffective representation and losing trial tactics. Indeed, counsel's performance will not be considered ineffective, even if unsuccessful, as long as it reflects an objectively reasonable trial strategy under the circumstances and evidence presented. "What constitutes effective assistance of counsel is not and cannot be fixed with yardstick precision, but varies according to the unique circumstances of each representation." People v. Benevento, 91 N.Y.2d at 712-713; People v. Satterfield, 66 N.Y.2d 796, 799 (1985).

When evaluating ineffective assistance of counsel claims, courts consider "whether counsel's conduct so undermined the proper functioning of the adversarial process that the trial cannot be relied on as having produced a just result." Strickland v. Washington, 466 U.S. 668, 686.

To make out an ineffective assistance of counsel claim under the federal constitution, a defendant must establish that counsel's performance was deficient, that the deficient performance prejudiced the defendant and thereby deprived the defendant of a fair trial and reliable result, and that counsel acted unreasonably under the prevailing professional norms. Prejudice is established if "[t]he defendant...show[s] that there is a reasonable probability that, but for counsel's unprofessional errors, the result of the proceeding would have been different. A reasonable probability is a probability sufficient to undermine confidence in the outcome." See Strickland v. Washington, 466 U.S. at 686-694.

One major difference between the New York standard and the standard announced in Strickland v. Washington, is the way the prejudice is analyzed. The New York Court of Appeals indicated that under the New York standard, the prejudice test of Strickland need not be fully satisfied, and that while a defendant's showing of prejudice is important, it not an "indispens[a]ble element in assessing meaningful representation." The Court of Appeals further noted that "[o]ur focus is on the fairness of the proceeding as a whole." People v. Stultz, 2 N.Y.3d 277, 284.

A. **TRIAL COUNSEL'S FAILURE TO CONTEST THE FORENSIC TESTING COULD NOT HAVE PRODUCED A JUST RESULT.**

In order to produce trustworthy results, analysts, among other things, must have sufficient expertise in forensic testing; they must handle samples in manners that ensure the samples' integrity; they must use dependable testing methods; they must interpret their data properly; and they must verify tentative conclusions by testing samples using at least **two different methods.** In the instant matter, the lab reports indicate that only **one method** was utilized. See Exhibits "F" and "G"; See United States Dep't of Justice, Drug Enforcement Administration & Executive

Office of the President, Office of National Drug Control Policy, Counterdrug Technology Assessment Center, Scientific Working Group for the Analysis of Seized Drugs (SWGDRUG) Recommendations, at 14-16 (3d ed.2007-08-09); Paul C. Gianelli, the Admissibility of Laboratory Reports in Criminal Trials: The Reliability of Scientific Proof, 49 Ohio St.L.J. 671, 688-695; See Also Project Advisory Committee, Laboratory Proficiency Testing Program, Supplementary Report - Samples 6-10, at 3 (1976) (finding that 30% of state forensic examiners asked to test a substance for the presence of cocaine rendered incorrect results).

Serious deficiencies have been found in the forensic evidence used in criminal trials. One commentator asserts that "[t]he legal community now concedes, with varying degrees of urgency, that our system produces erroneous convictions based on discredited forensics." Metzger, Cheating the Constitution, 59 Vand.L.Rev. 475, 491 (2006).

One study of cases in which exonerating evidence resulted in the overturning of criminal convictions concluded that invalid forensic testimony contributed to the **convictions in 60%** of the cases. Like expert witnesses generally, an analyst's lack of proper training or deficiency in judgment may be disclosed in cross-examination. Where, as here, defense trial counsel chose to forego that the state forensic analyst's evidentiary certification and lab reports be subject to the customary processes of direct and cross-examination, and it is clear that only one testing method was conducted, the trial cannot be said to have promoted a just result or the ends of justice. See 16 C.J.S. §2113, at 837-838 (1918) ("[Records are not admissible to prove the acts constituting the offense itself. Where a document or record relates to facts which are not such as can be proved only by an original or certified copy, but may be established by oral testimony... the constitutional guaranty [of confrontation] applies").

B. **TRIAL COUNSEL'S FAILURE TO CROSS-EXAMINE THE FORENSIC ANALYST IN THIS CASE DEPRIVED HIM OF HIS RIGHT TO DUE PROCESS.**

In the wake of the United States Supreme Court's decision in Crawford v. Washington, 541 U.S. 36 (2004), the Confrontation Clause returned to its traditional mode of operation - that is, to a procedural provision that forbids the government from introducing "testimonial" hearsay in place of live testimony at trial. A classic form of testimonial hearsay is an ex parte affidavit, and modern forensic laboratory certificates are the functional equivalent of such affidavits. See Crawford v. Washington, 541 U.S. 36 at 43-49, 124 S.Ct. 1354.

The Crawford opinion and the Supreme Court's subsequent decision in Davis v. Washington, 547 U.S. 813. (2006), both decided before the trial in this matter, "left for another day any effort to spell out a comprehensive definition of 'testimonial.'" Nonetheless, the Supreme Court had already provided considerable guidance concerning the concept. As a starting point, the Supreme Court had noted that "testimony" is "[a] solemn declaration or affirmation made for the purpose of establishing or proving some fact." The Court also emphasized that "the principal evil at which the Confrontation Clause was directed was the civil-law mode of criminal procedure: -particularly "its use of ex parte examinations" and "sworn ex parte affidavits" as substitutes for live testimony against the accused. Crawford v. Washington, 541 U.S. 36 at 50-52, n.3, quoting 2 Noah Webster, American Dictionary of the English Language (1828); See Also Dowdell v. United States, 221 U.S. 325, 330 (1911) (Confrontation Clause "intended to prevent the conviction of the accused upon depositions or ex parte affidavits"); Mattox v. United States, 156 U.S. 237, 242 (1895) (clause intended to prohibit use of "ex parte affidavits" in place of live testimony).

One of the elements of the crimes with which the defendant was charged was that he possessed four ounces of cocaine. In order to establish that element, the prosecution offered the forensic analyst's sworn certificate and the stipulation, and the jury was instructed that it could find the defendant possessed four ounces of cocaine based upon this "testimonial" evidence.

"[A] witness is considered to be a witness 'against' a defendant for purposes of the Confrontation Clause...if his testimony is part of the body of evidence that the jury may consider in assessing his guilt." Cruz v. New York, 481 U.S. 186, 198 (1987).

As the Supreme Court explained in Crawford, the Confrontation clause "commands, not that evidence be reliable, but that reliability be assessed in a particular manner: by testing in the crucible of cross-examination." Id. "Dispensing with confrontation because testimony is obviously reliable is akin to dispensing with jury trial because a defendant is obviously guilty. This is not what the Sixth Amendment prescribes." Id. at 62. Defendant had a right to insist that prosecutorial testimony be presented through the traditional adversarial process, but defense trial counsel waived that right and allowed the jury to accept the forensic analyst's reports and the erroneous stipulation as evidence that could form the basis of his conviction.

C. **DEFENSE COUNSEL'S STIPULATION ENTERED INTO WITH THE PROSECUTION RESULTED IN A PRESUMTPIVELY UNFAIR AND UNRELIABLE TRIAL.**

Counsel's most prejudicial error by far, was his entering into an erroneous stipulation with the prosecutor that contained information which is not factual.

The date that is stipulated to regarding when the analyst received the People's exhibit sealed from the evidence clerk at the lab could not serve as a proper foundation for the introduction of these reports into the trial. See People v. Klaus, 94 A.D.2d 748, 462 N.Y.S.2d 498 (1983); See Also Sinicropi v. Milone, 915 F.2d 66, 68 (2dCir.1990) (It is clear that a court is not always bound by a stipulation); PPX Enterprises, Inc. v. Audiofidelity, Inc., 746 F. 2d 120, 123 (2d Cir.1984) (Parties may not create a case by stipulating to facts that do not exist).

Defense counsel's failure to assert defendant's constitutional right to confront the witness against him in this case was further compounded by his entering into an erroneous stipulation with the prosecution. It further shows the poor preparation of counsel where the trial in this matter is concerned. These matters are obvious from the record, and there is no way for the defendant to discern what else may be inaccurate with regard to the testing methods that were employed by this analyst. Had counsel called him as a witness to testify he could have clarified any discrepancies that are clear from the record as well as those that aren't. Most importantly, if counsel would have objected to the introduction of the erroneous stipulation it could have been stricken before it was allowed to be used as evidence against the defendant in support of the prosecution's case.

Instead, defense counsel's erroneous stipulation entered into with the prosecution in this matter did not support defendant's defense or soften the damaging affidavit of the analyst that was admitted into evidence in direct contravention of defendant's right to confrontation. The erroneous stipulation only served to prejudice the defense and support the prosecution's trial theory that defendant was apprehended and found to be in possession of four ounces of cocaine.

Viewing these facts in conjunction with the numerous deficiencies in trial counsel's performance set out above, it is respectfully submitted that trial counsel had not become familiarized with the law and facts which pertain to my case enough to represent me properly, which resulted in a trial performance amounting to a constructive denial of counsel altogether. Still, even if his performance were somehow above that level, it was still below an objective standard of reasonableness, and there is a reasonable probability that, but for counsel's unprofessional errors, the result of defendant's trial would have been different.

GROUND III

DEFENSE TRIAL COUNSEL SHOULD BE ORDERED TO SUBMIT AN AFFIDAVIT RESPONDING TO THE ALLEGATIONS IN THIS MOTION.

An inquiry into defense counsel's conversations with his client may be critical to a proper assessment of counsel's investigative decisions, as well as other litigation decisions. Because the contents of the conversations are not normally a part of the record on direct appeal, claims of ineffective assistance of trial counsel are more properly raised on a post-conviction motion pursuant to C.P.L. §440.10. See Yael v. Levy, Federal Review of Procedural Bars To Ineffective Assistance Claims, N.Y.L.J., pp. 4, 8 (October 5, 2009), citing People v. Brown, 28 N.Y.2d 282, 287 (1971).

During the litigation of such a proceeding, the reduction of burdens to all concerned, and the interests of judicial time and economy would be better served "through the use of affidavits or other simplifying procedures" as a prelude to an evidentiary hearing. Murray v. Carrier, 477 U.S. 478, 487, 106 S.Ct. 2639, 2645 (1986). The issues needed to be developed at the hearing may be narrowed drastically in this manner.

A defendant must submit "an affidavit from the attorney who represented him at trial or offer an explanation of his failure to do so before he can assert an entitlement to an evidentiary hearing." People v. Morales, 58 N.Y.2d 1008, 1009, 461 N.Y.S.2d 1011, 1012 (1983).

The defendant has written to defense trial counsel inquiring as to why he waived his constitutional right to confront witnesses, and why he failed to file an appeal on the defendant's behalf. However, he has refused to respond. Additionally, the defendant has sent trial counsel a letter, accompanied by these motion papers and exhibits, asking him to provide the court, district attorney, and defendant with the necessary affidavit. Exhibits "H" and "I".

This motion's return date is set for over 30 days from the date of the letter. That should be enough time for trial counsel to provide the requested affidavit. People v. Scott, 10 N.Y.2d 380, 382, 223 N.Y.S.2d 472, 473-474 (1961).

In the event that he does not provide the affidavit by then, it would be appropriate for the court to issue an order directing him to do so.

The affidavit sought herein is extremely material to a determination of this motion. Consequently, the court has clear authority under Judiciary Law, §2-b(3), to direct defense counsel to submit an affidavit, and authority under C.P.L.R. §1101 and §1102 to assign an attorney to represent the defendant and obtain the necessary affidavits in this matter.

Indeed, if affidavits are so 'necessary' that a pro se defendant's failure to at least try to obtain them on his own behalf would warrant the dismissal of his motion, it follows that such affidavits would be just as "necessary to carry into effect the powers and jurisdiction possessed by the court" to justify the court in taking whatever steps may be required to have them submitted under Judiciary Law, §2-b(3).

WHEREFORE, petitioner respectfully prays that this court make an order granting the relief sought herein, and granting such other and further relief as to the court may be just, proper and equitable.

        Respectully submitted,

        _____

        _____ # _____
        Petitioner Pro Se
        Gowanda Correctional Facility
        P.O. Box 311
        Gowanda, NY 14070

Sworn to before me this

_____ day of _____, 20___,

_____

GORILLA LAWFAIR   71

(SAMPLE LETTER)

_____ #_____
_____ Corr. Facility
_____
_____

_____, ____, 20__

_____, Esq.
_____
_____
_____

Re: People v. (Defendant's Name)

Dear counsel:

After reviewing the records that I have obtained in my case, I learned that you entered into a stipulation with the Assistant District Attorney regarding the credentials and results of the drug testing done by the analyst in my case. The question I would like to ask is why did you waive my right to confrontation with regard to the prosecution witness and his findings when my case centers around drug possession?

The Sixth Amendment to the U.S. Constitution guarantees a criminal defendant the right "to be confronted with the witnesses against him." Prior to your representation of my case in this matter, Crawford v. Washington was decided by the United States Supreme Court. Under Crawford, a witness's testimony against a defendant is inadmissible unless the witness appears at trial, or if the witness is unavailable, the defendant had a prior opportunity for cross-examination. The certificate that was prepared by the analyst in my case and introduced at my trial is an affidavit which falls within the "core class of testimonial statements" covered by the Confrontation Clause. Therefore, I was entitled to be confronted with the person(s) giving testimony at my trial through these testimonial statements.

Since you never informed me that you were going to waive my constitutional right to confrontation, could you please tell me why? Also, I recently learned that you never filed an appeal of my case to the Second Department and I would like to know why you chose not to do that as well.

Very truly yours,

_____

SUPREME COURT OF THE STATE OF NEW YORK COUNTY
OF _____
--X

The People of the State of New York

                          (BLANK)
      Plaintiffs,   **NOTICE OF MOTION TO**
      -against-   **VACATE JUDGEMENT**

_____,

Defendant.
                         IND NO._____
--X

PLEASE TAKE NOTICE, that upon the annexed affidavit of _____, sworn to on the _____ day of _____, 20____, and all the documents attached thereto, and upon the accusatory instrument and all of the proceedings had herein, the Defendant will move this Court, at Part _____ thereof, at the Courthouse located at _____, on the _____ day of _____, 20____ at 9:30 a.m., or as soon thereafter as counsel may be heard for:

(1) an Order, pursuant to Criminal Procedure Law §440.10(1)(h), vacating the Judgment heretofore entered upon the above named defendant on the _____ day of _____, 20____, or

in the alternative, ordering a hearing to determine whether such judgment should be vacated on the grounds that:

_____
_____
_____
_____

(2) Defendant is currently confined at _____, and it is requested that the Court, pursuant to New York Criminal Procedure Law §440.30(5), cause the defendant who is confined as hereinabove stated, to be produced at any hearing which the Court shall conduct to determine this motion; and

(3) Such other and further relief as to the Court may seem just and proper.

PLEASE TAKE FURTHER NOTICE, that pursuant to C.P.L.R. §2214(b), answering affidavits, if any, are required to be served upon the undersigned at least seven (7) days before the return date of this motion.

Dated: _____, ____, 20__ .
             _____, New York

TO: _____   _____
District Attorney   Defendant Pro Se
_____ County   _____
_____, New York   _____

SUPREME COURT OF THE STATE OF NEW YORK COUNTY
OF _____
--X

The People of the State of New York

        Plaintiffs,   **AFFIDAVIT IN SUPPORT**
                            OF MOTION TO VACATE
       -against-   **JUDGMENT**

_____,

Defendant.
                              IND NO._____
--X
STATE OF NEW YORK   )
)ss.:
COUNTY OF   )

_____, being duly sworn, deposes and says:

1. I am the defendant herein, and I am currently incarcerated at _____.

2. I make this affidavit in support of my motion pursuant to CPL §440.10(1)(h) of New York Criminal Procedure Law for an order vacating the Judgment of conviction in the above entitled matter upon the ground(s) that:

(1) _____
_____
_____

(2) _____
_____
_____

3. This affidavit is also made in support of my requests **(a)** for a order pursuant to Judiciary Law §2-b[3], directing attorney _____, Esq., to serve and file an affidavit responding to the allegations made hereinafter about his trial performance on the ground that such a responding affidavit is necessary to carry into effect the powers and jurisdiction possessed by the Court, and to better serve the interests of judicial time and economy; (b) for an order pursuant to C.P.L.R. §1101 and §1102 assigning an attorney to represent me in this proceeding on the ground that I cannot afford such professional services needed to argue the merits of my issues for a proper determination of my motion to vacate judgment; (c) for an order pursuant to C.P.L. §440.30(5), granting an evidentiary hearing on the ground that one is essential to create the evidentiary record necessary for the Court to adequately, effectively and meaningfully determine my motion to vacate judgment; and **(d)** for an order granting defendant's motion to vacate judgment; and (e) for an order granting such other and further relief as to the Court may seem just and proper.

PROCEDURAL HISTORY

I was indicted by a _____ County grand jury charging defendant with _____, and convicted before Hon. _____, Judge, after a jury trial during which I didn't testify (guilty plea). I was represented by attorney _____. Said conviction was for _____.

4. _____
_____
_____
_____
_____

5. No previous application for the relief sought herein has been made to this or any other Court.

FACTS

6. _____
_____
_____
_____
_____
_____
_____

7. _____
_____
_____
_____
_____

WHEREFORE, petitioner requests that this honorable Court, pursuant to New York Criminal Procedure Law §440.30(5), cause the defendant who is confined at _____ to be produced at any hearing which the Court shall conduct to determine this motion; and that under C.P.L.R. §1101 and §1102, as well as County Law §722, assign suitable counsel to represent the defendant in this matter.

Respectfully submitted,

_____

_____ # _____

Petitioner Pro Se

_____ Correctional Facility

_____

_____ NY _____

Sworn to before me this _____ day of _____ 20___.

_____

SUPREME COURT OF THE STATE OF NEW YORK COUNTY
OF _____
--X

The People of the State of New York
                                    (SAMPLE)
    Plaintiffs,   **NOTICE OF MOTION TO**
                            SET ASIDE SENTENCE
   -against-

_____,

Defendant.
                                IND NO._____
--X

    PLEASE TAKE NOTICE, that upon the annexed affidavit of _____, sworn to on the _____ day of _____, 20___, and all the documents attached thereto, and upon the accusatory instrument and all of the proceedings had herein, the defendant will move this Court at Part _____ thereof, at the Courthouse located at 100 Centre Street, New York, NY 10010 on the _____ day of _____, 20___ at 9:30 a.m., or as soon thereafter as counsel may be heard for:
    (1) an order pursuant to Criminal Procedure Law §440.20, setting aside the sentence heretofore imposed upon the above named defendant on the 31st day of March, 1998, or in the alternative, ordering a

hearing to determine whether such sentence should be set aside on the grounds that:

Defendant's Sentence Was The Product Of A Plea Bargain Which Made His Sentence Concurrent To Time Owed On A Previously Imposed Federal Sentence, And That Because Federal Authorities Didn't Take Custody Of Defendant Until His Conditional Release From His New York Sentence, Defendant's New York Sentence Is In Fact Being Served Consecutively To His Federal Sentence In Violation Of The Defendant's Right To Due Process Of Law Under The Constitution Of This State And The United States. N.Y. Const., Article I, §6; U.S. Const., XIV Amend.

(2) Defendant is currently confined at _____

_____ and it is requested that the Court, pursuant to New York Criminal Procedure Law §440.30(5), cause the defendant who is confined as hereinabove stated, to be produced at any hearing which the Court shall conduct to determine this motion; and

(3) Such other and further relief as to the Court may seem just and proper.

PLEASE TAKE FURTHER NOTICE, that pursuant to C.P.L.R. §2214(b), answering affidavits, if any, are required to be served upon the undersigned at least seven (7) days before the return date of this motion.

Dated: _____, ____, 20__.
       _____, New York

TO: _____   _____
District Attorney   Defendant Pro Se
_____County   _____
_____, New York   _____
                                 _____

SUPREME COURT OF THE STATE OF NEW YORK COUNTY OF _____
--X

The People of the State of New York
                              (SAMPLE)
        Plaintiffs,   **AFFIDAVIT IN SUPPORT**
                         OF MOTION TO SET ASIDE
        -against-   **SENTENCE**
_____,

Defendant.
                         IND NO._____
--X
STATE OF NEW YORK   )
)ss.:
COUNTY OF   )

_____, being duly sworn, deposes and says:

1. I am the defendant in the above entitled proceeding and I make this affidavit in support of a motion pursuant to §440.20 of the New York Criminal Procedure Law to set aside the sentence heretofore imposed by Hon Judge _____, of the New York County Supreme Court on March 31, 1998 upon the ground(s) that:

DEFENDANT'S PLEA BARGAIN WAS THE PRODUCT OF A PLEA BARGAIN WHICH MADE HIS SENTENCE CONCURRENT TO TIME OWED ON A PREVIOUSLY IMPOSED FEDERAL SENTENCE, AND THAT BECAUSE FEDERAL AUTHORITIES DIDN'T TAKE CUSTODY OF DEFENDANT UNTIL HIS CONDITIONAL RELEASE

FROM HIS NEW YORK SENTENCE, DEFENDANT'S NEW YORK SENTENCE IS IN FACT BEING SERVED CONSECUTIVELY TO HIS FEDERAL SENTENCE IN VIOLATION OF THE DEFENDANT'S RIGHT TO DUE PROCESS OF LAW UNDER THE CONSTITUTION OF THIS STATE AND OF THE UNITED STATES.

2. I was indicted for criminal use of a firearm 1°, attempted murder 2°, assault 1°, attempted robbery 1°, and criminal possession of a weapon 2°.

3. Federal authorities obtained defendant from state authorities on January 13, 1997 via a writ of habeas corpus ad prosequendum, and transported him to Virginia for trial on a federal indictment charging him with bank robbery and use of a firearm during a crime of violence. The United States District Court for the Western District of Virginia sentenced the defendant on February 12, 1998 to 60 months of imprisonment on each of the bank robbery counts, with the sentences to run concurrently with each other; and to 60 months of imprisonment on the firearm offense to run consecutively to all other sentences. Following sentencing, federal authorities returned defendant to state authorities on March 8, 1998 and the federal judgments were filed with state authorities as a detainer on April 26, 1998. See Exhibits "E" and "H" annexed.

4. After plea negotiations, the defendant was allowed to enter a plea of guilty to the charge of criminal possession of a weapon in the second degree. At the sentencing hearing

conducted on March 31, 1998, defendant's counsel stated on the record to the court: "I rely on the promise of [seven and a half to fifteen years], but I know it is a little more complicated, as usual, insofar as he is in federal prison right now, as well. I have the number of the case in which he is serving federal time, 3:96-00100." The sentencing Judge then stated that "the sentence of the Court is, as promised, seven and a half to fifteen years, that sentence is to run concurrent with the federal sentence as referred to as case No. 3:96-00100." See Exhibit "C" annexed.

5. Rather than designate that the defendant be returned to the "appropriate official," i.e., the federal authorities, the court clerk mistakenly committed the defendant to the custody of the New York State Department of Correctional Services [NYSDOCS], now Department of Corrections and Community Service [DOCCS], in direct contravention to Penal Law §70.20(3) and §70.30(2-a). The defendant was received unlawfully by DOCCS on April 22, 1998. DOCCS paroled the defendant from the State term on January 23, 2006 and on January 24, 2006 the United States Marshals Service [USMS] received defendant into federal custody.

6. The Bureau of Prisons [BOP] prepared a sentence computation for defendant commencing the total 120 month sentence on January 24, 2006. The BOP credited defendant with 39 days and informed him that he would have to serve

his federal sentence consecutively to his New York State concurrent sentence. See Page 2 of Exhibit "H".

7. Petitioner then filed a petition for a writ of habeas corpus pursuant to 28 U.S.C. §2241 in the United States District Court for the Southern District of Florida seeking release from custody on the ground that his New York sentence is concurrent with his previously imposed federal sentence. In its decision denying defendant's petition, the District Court noted that the BOP National Inmate Appeals Department considered whether a nunc pro tunc designation to the New York City Department of Corrections [NYCDOC] would be appropriate in the defendant's case. However, "despite being contacted by the BOP, the state sentencing judge had not responded with any statement in favor of granting a nunc pro tunc designation regarding petitioner's federal term of confinement."[3]

8. The District Court went on further to state that the "imposition of the state sentence as concurrent to the federal sentence did not accomplish a change of primary jurisdiction," and that: "As he has already served his time of confinement

---

[3] Defendant, being a layman at law who is also further disadvantaged by not having access to New York Law materials to conduct research into this matter is in desperate need of judicial intervention and respectfully requests that this honorable Court contact the BOP National Inmate Appeals Department with a statement in favor of granting a nunc pro tunc designation regarding the concurrency of defendant's federal term of confinement.

on the state sentence, however, there is no remedy that this court can provide regarding the execution of his state sentence." The District Court ultimately dismissed defendant's petition. As a result, the defendant is currently serving his 120 month federal sentence consecutively to his New York sentence. See Exhibit "H" at pp. 3, 6, and 7.

ARGUMENT

GROUND I

THE CLERK OF THE COURT DEPRIVED DEFENDANT OF HIS DUE PROCESS RIGHT TO SERVE HIS STATE SENTENCE CONCURRENTLY WITH HIS UNDISCHARGED FEDERAL SENTENCE BY ISSUING A COMMITMENT THAT DEPARTED FROM THE JUDGE'S ORAL PRONOUNCEMENT THAT DEFENDANT'S SENTENCE WAS CONCURRENT WITH HIS FEDERAL SENTENCE. U.S. CONST., XIV AMEND; N.Y. CONST., ART. I, §6.

Under New York Penal Law §70.20(3) and 70.30(2-a), "when a defendant who is subject to an undischarged term of imprisonment, imposed at a previous time by a court of another jurisdiction is sentenced to an additional term or terms of imprisonment by a court of this state to run concurrently with such undischarged term as provided in subdivision four of section 70.25, the return of the defendant to the custody of the appropriate official of the other jurisdiction shall be deemed a commitment for such portion of the term or terms of the sentence imposed by the court of this state as shall not exceed the said undischarged term."

In the instant matter, the sentence imposed by the court was an indeterminate term of 7½ years to 15 years. "That sentence to run concurrent with the federal sentence as referred to as case No. 3:96-00100," However, after the conclusion of the sentencing proceedings, the clerk of the court issued an order committing defendant to the custody of DOCCS rather than the federal authorities. Since the defendant was not returned to the custody of the federal authorities, his New York sentence and his federal sentence did not begin to run as directed by the judge, and the defendant is faced with having to serve his federal term consecutively to his New York State term. This increase of the defendant's sentence by an additional 120 months is unconstitutional and deprived him of his constitutional right to due process of law. People v. Karney, 160 A.D.2d 1025 (2d Dept.1990).

"[T]he sentence imposed by a sentencing judge is controlling; it is this sentence that constitutes the court's judgment and authorizes custody of the defendant." Hill v. United States ex rel. Wampler, 298 U.S. 450 (1935).

The goal of seeking to protect the defendant's due process rights where matters of commitment are concerned was displayed in Wampler wherein the clerk of the court pursuant to custom, added a condition to the defendant's sentence of eighteen months and a $5,000 fine. Specifically, that the defendant was to remain in custody until the fine was paid. In holding that the clerk did not have the power to alter the sentence imposed by the court by way of a "warrant of commitment," Justice Cardozo opined that "the only sentence known to the law is the sentence or judgment entered upon the records of the court...until corrected in a direct proceeding, it says what it was meant to say, and this is by an irrebuttable presumption." The court in Wampler, therefore excluded a "warrant of commitment" prepared by the clerk of the court. Hill v. United States ex rel. Wampler, 298 U.S. at 464.

Petitioner asserts that the holding of Wampler also applies to a case, such as the instant matter where the court clerk's commitment departed from the trial judge's oral pronouncement of sentence. And that due to this error, defendant's sentence had not "commenced" under Penal Law §70.30(2-a).

Because the court sentenced defendant to concurrent sentences, his sentence should be reduced to the legal minimum of 2 years to 4 years with a new commitment order issued committing defendant to the federal authorities so that defendant's sentence will comport with the intent of the original plea bargain. Santobello v. New York, 404 U.S. 257 (1971); See Also Exhibit "I" annexed. The gravamen of defendant's argument is that he is entitled to concurrent sentences. Bureau of Prison officials apparently also thought that the sentence was meant to be served concurrently because, according to BOP, "despite being contacted by the BOP, the state sentencing judge had not responded with any statement in favor of granting a nunc pro tunc designation regarding petitioner's federal term of confinement. Since the court sentenced defendant to concurrent terms, and he is serving consecutive terms his sentence should be reduced. Further, the court should contact the BOP with a statement in favor of granting a concurrent nunc pro tunc designation regarding defendant's federal term of confinement.[4] People v. Bogan, 63 A.D.2d 582 (1st Dept.1978) ("where a court cannot exactly comply with the terms of a plea bargain, it should conform the sentence to the promise as closely as practicable"); 18 U.S.C. §3621(b); See Also page 3 of Exhibit "H".

If, as in Wampler, an erroneous order of commitment prepared by the clerk of the court with the court's knowledge cannot alter the

---

[4] **NOTE:** It can also be requested of the court to conform the sentence of an individual currently in NYS custody with an order that they be sent to the "appropriate authorities" of the other jurisdiction whether it be federal or state.

sentence imposed by the court, then here, a later addition by the clerk of the court without the court's knowledge cannot do it. "Only the judgment of a court, as expressed through the sentence imposed by a judge has the power to constrain a person's liberty. See Hill v. United States-ex rel. Wampler, 298 U.S. at 464 ("In any collateral inquiry, a court will close its ears to a suggestion that the sentence entered in the minutes is something other than the authentic expression of the sentencing judge").

The interpretation of federal constitutional law by a lower federal court is persuasive but not binding authority on New York Courts." People v. Kin Kan, 78 N.Y.2d 54 (1991). However, the Fourteenth Amendment and the Supremacy Clause of the Federal Constitution make the United States Supreme Court's interpretation of this matter binding authority. U.S. Const., Art. VI, cl. 2.

Since defendant was never sentenced consecutively by the nisi prius court during the sentencing phase of his New York state conviction, and since the actions of the clerk of the court deprived the defendant of his due process right to serve his state sentence concurrently with his undischarged federal sentence by issuing a commitment that deprived him of the judge's oral pronouncement that defendant's sentence was concurrent with his federal sentence, he asks that this honorable court adopt and apply Wampler to his application and (1) set aside the sentence and resentence defendant to the legal minimum of 2 years to 4 years with a new commitment order issued committing defendant to the federal authorities so that defendant's sentence will comport with the intent of the plea bargain; (2) contact the BOP National Inmate Appeals Department with a statement in favor of granting a nunc pro tunc designation regarding the concurrency of defendant's federal term of confinement; and for such other and further relief as to this court may seem just, proper and equitable.

CONCLUSION

For the reasons stated above, defendant's sentence should be vacated and he should be granted the relief sought.[5]

The grounds for relief described by this affidavit have not been determined on the merits upon a prior motion or proceeding in a court of this state, or upon a prior motion or proceeding in a Federal court.

WHEREFORE, petitioner further requests that the court, pursuant to New York Criminal Procedure Law §440.30(5), cause the defendant who is confined at _____

---

[5] Resentencing defendant and committing him to federal custody for service of his concurrent sentences should allow defendant to receive prior custody credit. Defendant cannot currently receive more than the 39 day prior time he was granted by BOP because it was already credited to him previously by DOCCS. See United States v. Wilson, 503 U.S. 329, 337 (1992); See Also 18 U.S.C. §3585(b).

to be produced at any hearing which the Court shall conduct to determine this motion; and that under C.P.L.R. §1101 and §1102, as well as County Law §722, assign suitable counsel to represent the defendant in this matter.

        Respectfully submitted,

        _____

        _____ #_____
        Petitioner Pro Se
        _____ Correctional Facility

        _____

        _____ NY _____

Sworn to before me this
_____ day of _____ 20____.

_____

SUPREME COURT OF THE STATE OF NEW YORK COUNTY OF _____

------------------------------------X

The People of the State of New York

                                 (BLANK)
      Plaintiffs,   **NOTICE OF MOTION TO**
                           SET ASIDE SENTENCE
     -against-

_____,

Defendant.

                             IND NO._____

------------------------------------X

    PLEASE TAKE NOTICE, that upon the annexed affidavit of _____, sworn to on the ____ day of _____, 20___, and all the documents attached thereto, and upon the accusatory instrument and all of the proceedings had herein, the defendant will move this Court, at Part _____ thereof, at the Courthouse located at _____, on the _____ day of _____, 20___ at 9:30 a.m., or as soon thereafter as counsel may be heard for:

    (1) an order pursuant to Criminal Procedure Law §440.20 setting aside the sentence heretofore imposed upon the above named defendant on the _____ day of_____, 20___,

or in the alternative, ordering a hearing to determine whether such sentence should be set aside on the grounds that:

_____
_____
_____
_____

(2) Defendant is currently confined at _____, and it is requested that the Court, pursuant to New York Criminal Procedure Law §440.30(5) cause the defendant who is confined as hereinabove stated, to be produced at any hearing which the Court shall conduct to determine this motion; and

(3) such other and further relief as to the Court may seem just and proper.

PLEASE TAKE FURTHER NOTICE, that pursuant to C.P.L.R. §2214(b), answering affidavits, if any, are required to be served upon the undersigned at least seven (7) days before the return date of this motion.

Dated: _____, ____, 20__.
_____, New York

TO: _____   _____
District Attorney   Defendant Pro Se
_____ County   _____
_____, New York   _____
                           _____

SUPREME COURT OF THE STATE OF NEW YORK COUNTY OF _____
--X

The People of the State of New York

        Plaintiffs,   **AFFIDAVIT IN SUPPORT OF MOTION TO VACATE**
        -against-   **JUDGMENT**

_____,

Defendant.
                       IND NO._____
--X
STATE OF NEW YORK   )
)ss.:
COUNTY OF   )

_____, being duly sworn, deposes and says:

1. I am the defendant in the above entitled proceeding and I make this affidavit in support of a motion pursuant to §440.20 of the New York Criminal Procedure Law to set aside the sentence heretofore imposed by Hon. Judge _____, of the _____ County Supreme Court on _____ _____, 20____, upon the ground that:

_____
_____
_____
_____

2. This criminal proceeding commenced pursuant to an indictment that was filed in _____ county charging the defendant with _____.
At my arraignment I pleaded not guilty. Bail was set at $_____.

3. After a jury (bench) trial a verdict of guilty was rendered against me on the following charge(s): _____
_____.

Or (After plea negotiations the defendant was allowed to enter a plea of guilty to the charge(s) of: _____
_____.

4. I was sentenced to a/an determinate/indeterminate term of imprisonment, i.e., _____,
before the Hon. Judge _____,
in Part _____ of the _____ County Supreme Court.

GROUNDS FOR RELIEF

5. _____
_____
_____
_____

CONCLUSION

For the reasons stated above, defendant's sentences should be vacated and he should be granted the relief sought.

The grounds for relief described in this affidavit have not been determined on the merits upon a prior motion or proceeding in a federal court.

WHEREFORE, petitioner further requests that the court, pursuant to New York Criminal Procedure Law §440.30(5), cause the defendant who is confined at _____,
to be produced at any hearing which the Court shall conduct to determine this motion; and that under C.P.L.R. §1101 and §1102, as well as County Law §722, assign suitable counsel to represent the defendant in this matter.

        Respectfully submitted,

        _____

        _____ # _____
        Petitioner Pro Se

        _____ Correctional Facility

        _____

        _____ NY _____

Sworn to before me this
_____ day of _____ 20____.
_____

POSTCONVICTION REMEDIES

The writ of error coram nobis is a common-law remedy to raise ineffective assistance of counsel in the proper appellate court. Under New York law there is no statutory remedy available to advance such a claim. The right to the effective assistance of counsel is guaranteed under the Federal and State Constitutions. Therefore, the New York Court of Appeals has concluded that "the natural venue for coram nobis review of ineffective assistance of appellate counsel claims is in the appellate tribunal where the alleged deficient representation occurred." People v. Bachert, 69 N.Y.2d 593, 516 N.Y.S.2d 623 (1987).

In order to prevail on a claim of ineffective assistance of appellate counsel, the individual raising the claim has to first show that the issues which were not raised by counsel on appeal were apparent from the record. In other words, the lawyer should have known from a brief review of the record that the issue(s) in question would have likely resulted in a reversal or modification, and there is no legal justification for counsel not raising them on appeal. People v. Rutter, 202 A.D.2d 123, 616 N.Y.S.2d 598 (1994).

As we have pointed out in our Sample Motion For Writ of Error Coram Nobis, under the federal standard for ineffective assistance of counsel claims, a two-part test must be satisfied. First, the appellant "must show that his attorney's performance 'fell below an objective standard of reasonableness,' and second, he must show that there is a 'reasonable probability' that but for counsel's errors, the outcome would have been different." Mayo v. Henderson, 13 F.3d 528 (2d Cir.1994).

If you are going to allege that appellate counsel was ineffective for failure to raise a particular claim you should contact the appellate attorney in the form of a letter sent certified-mail, return-receipt requested with a Affidavit of Service requesting that the attorney explain their failure to raise a colorable claim that was apparent in the face of the record. If counsel communicates back to you the letter may be able to aid you in substantiating your claim. Some attorneys will give an honest response when questioned regarding an omission on their part. In a lot of cases, appellate attorneys do not respond to such inquiries. However, regardless of the outcome you should always show the court that you made the attempt to communicate with appellate counsel regarding the issue(s) whether you receive a response or not.

WHERE TO FILE A CORAM NOBIS PETITION

A writ of error coram nobis must be filed in the appellate division where your appeal was decided. A copy of these documents must also be filed with the district attorney of the county where the judgment you are appealing was obtained.

WHAT TO FILE

(1) Cover letter to the court clerk explaining exactly what papers you are forwarding to the appellate division along with your letter.
(2) Notice of Motion for Writ of Error Coram Nobis.
(3) Affidavit in Support of Motion for Writ of Error Coram Nobis.
(4) Memorandum of Law.
(5) Affidavit of Service.

We have provided Sample Forms and Blank Forms to show the Error Coram Nobis Format.

WHAT TO EXPECT AFTER YOU FILE

After your papers are received by the appellate division and the district attorney's office, the district attorney will more than likely file papers in opposition to your motion stating why they feel you shouldn't be granted the relief you are seeking. You will be served with a copy of the Answer submitted by the district attorney and you should respond as promptly as possible. After all of the papers are received, the appellate division will render its decision. Writ of error applications are rarely granted, however, the advantage of filing one on the state level is that it gives an appellant the opportunity to seek a reversal or modification of their issue(s), and also allows them to preserve them for federal review. In the event that you file a petition and it is denied the next step is to seek leave to appeal to the Court of Appeals.

ADDRESSES TO THE APPELLATE COURTS IN NEW YORK STATE

Appellate Division
First Department
27 Madison Avenue
New York, NY 10010

Appellate Division
Second Department
45 Monroe Place
Brooklyn, NY 11201

Appellate Division
Third Department
Capitol Station
PO Box 7288
Albany, NY 12224-0288

Appellate Division
Fourth Department
50 East Avenue
Rochester, NY 14604-2214

SUPREME COURT OF THE STATE OF NEW YORK
APPELLATE DIVISION: _____ DEPARTMENT
_____

THE PEOPLE OF THE STATE OF NEW YORK,
    Respondent,   _____ COUNTY
    -against-
_____ #_____ IND. NO. _____
    Defendant-Appellant
_____

(SAMPLE)
WRIT OF ERROR CORAM NOBIS
FOR
APPELLANT-PETITIONER

_____
APPELLANT PRO SE
_____ Correctional Facility
_____
_____

SUPREME COURT OF THE STATE OF NEW YORK COUNTY OF _____
--X

The People of the State of New York
                                      (SAMPLE)
       Plaintiffs,   **NOTICE OF MOTION FOR**
                                    WRIT OF ERROR CORAM
      -against-   **NOBIS**

_____,

Defendant-Appellant.
                                    IND NO._____
--X

     PLEASE TAKE NOTICE, that upon the annexed affidavit of _____ _____ sworn to on the _____ day of _____, 20____, and all the documents attached thereto, and upon the proceedings heretofore had herein, appellant will move this Court at a term thereof to be held at the Appellate Division, _____ Department Courthouse located at _____, on the _____ day of _____, 20____ at ten o'clock in the forenoon of that day, or as soon thereafter as counsel may be heard for an Order vacating the _____, _____, 20____, Decision and Order of this Court affirming his conviction, and granting such other and further relief as may be just and proper upon the ground that he was denied his right to the effective assistance of counsel under the Fifth, Sixth, and Fourteenth Amendments of the United States Constitution on his direct appeal to this Court because:

(a) the assistance provided by his appellate counsel was so nominal it amounted to the substantial equivalent of being assigned no counsel at all; and

(b) if the assistance of appellate counsel was something more than nominal, it still did not reach a level of performance sufficient to satisfy an objective standard of reasonableness, and there is a 'reasonable probability' that but for counsel's deficient performance, the outcome of the appeal would have been different.

PLEASE TAKE FURTHER NOTICE, this motion is in the nature of Error Coram Nobis, and the answering papers, if any, shall be filed with proof of service on the undersigned at least seven (7) days before the return date of this motion in accordance with the provisions of C.P.L.R. §2214. This motion is submitted on the papers and personal appearance in opposition to the motion is neither required nor permitted.

Dated: _____, ____, 20__.
_____, New York

Respectfully submitted,

_____
_____ #_____
Petitioner Pro Se
_____ Correctional Facility
_____
_____ NY _____

TO: _____
_____ County District Attorney
_____
_____, NY _____

SUPREME COURT OF THE STATE OF NEW YORK COUNTY OF _____

------------------------------------X

The People of the State of New York

        Plaintiffs,   **AFFIDAVIT IN SUPPORT OF MOTION FOR A WRIT**

       -against-   **OF ERROR CORAM NOBIS**

_____,

Defendant-Appellant.

                       IND NO. _____

------------------------------------X

STATE OF NEW YORK   )
)ss.:
COUNTY OF _____)

_____, being duly sworn, deposes and says:

1. I am the above named defendant-appellant, am 18 years of age or older, and am currently incarcerated in the _____.

2. I make this affidavit in support of the instant motion for a writ of error coram nobis to vacate the _____, _____, 20___ Decision and Order of this Court affirming my conviction in the above matter. The basis of this motion is that I was deprived of my right to the effective assistance of counsel under the 5th, 6th, and 14th Amendments of the United States Constitution, and Article I, §6 of the New

York State Constitution upon my direct appeal to this Court from a judgment of conviction entered against me in the Supreme Court, County of _____,
on _____ _____, 20___
in that:

(a) THE ASSISTANCE PROVIDED BY MY APPELLATE COUNSEL WAS SO NOMINAL IT AMOUNTED TO THE SUBSTANTIAL EQUIVALENT OF BEING ASSIGNED NO COUNSEL AT ALL; and

(b) IF THE ASSISTANCE OF APPELLATE COUNSEL WAS SOMETHING MORE THAN NOMINAL, IT STILL DID NOT REACH A LEVEL OF PERFORMANCE SUFFICIENT TO SATISFY AN OBJECTIVE STANDARD OF REASONABLENESS, AND THERE IS A 'REASONABLE PROBABILITY' THAT BUT FOR COUNSEL'S DEFICIENT PERFORMANCE, THE OUTCOME OF MY DIRECT APPEAL WOULD HAVE BEEN DIFFERENT.

PROCEDURAL HISTORY

3. I was charged by indictment _____ and convicted in Supreme Court, County of _____, before Honorable (Judge's Name) after a jury trial.

4. On _____, _____, 20___ Judge _____ sentenced me to an indeterminate term of 25 years to life.

5. I filed a timely notice of appeal and poor person application, and this Court assigned (Lawyer's Name), Esq., to perfect the appeal on my behalf.

6. This Court affirmed my conviction in a published opinion dated _____, _____,
20___. See People v. Me, _____ N.Y.S.3d _____. I then applied to the New York State Court of Appeals for leave to appeal from this Court's Order of affirmance. That application was denied on _____ _____,
20___. See Exhibit "A".

7. No prior application has been made to any Court to review the adequacy of the representation I received upon my direct appeal to this Court.

FACTS
THE TRIAL

8. On November 8, 2007 the date of appellant's arrest, Officer Freeman who was assigned to the anti-crime unit of the 79th precinct was working at 6:00 p.m. to 2:00 a.m. tour of duty. Freeman was in plain clothes and riding in an unmarked police vehicle with police officer Mobley who was the driver. See T.T. 5. [All references indicated as T.T. are the appropriate pages of the trial transcript annexed hereto as Exhibit B].

9. According to Freeman, at approximately 11:18 p.m., they were in the vicinity of the Lafayette Gardens Housing Complex on Lafayette Avenue and Franklin Avenue when he observed an individual attempt to enter the vehicle, but that she fled and the individual in the driver's seat sped off in the car,

drove on to the sidewalk, and made a right turn on Franklin Avenue. T.T. 6-7.

10. The fleeing vehicle struck another vehicle that was crossing the intersection at Franklin Avenue and Clifton Place. The driver then exited the vehicle and fled. Freeman then chased after appellant, he observed him take a bag from his waistband and toss it into a pile of garbage bags. After arresting appellant he returned to recover the item that had been thrown away and found a large white ziplock bag inside of which was another sand-which like bag tied in a knot containing a white substance and tubular-type packaging. He then took these items to the property clerk at the precinct where it received Voucher Number B123456, and sent to the police laboratory for analysis. T.T. 8-18.

11. Sgt. Waters testified that he was the supervising officer of the anti-crime unit on November 8, 2007. After arriving to the scene of appellant's arrest, officer Freeman and officer Mobley informed him that they had arrested appellant after finding him to be in possession of a white rocky substance.

Stipulation

12. Unknown to appellant was the fact that the prosecutor and defense counsel entered into a stipulation concerning what the forensic analyst would testify to if he were called to testify at the trial. Also unknown to appellant was the fact that

defense counsel waived his right to confront the analyst after he told appellant that the analyst would be called to testify at the trial. Rather than have the analyst testify, defense counsel chose to allow the stipulation to enter into the trial although it contained erroneous information that would have amounted to the analyst perjuring himself if he testified to the erroneous stipulation.

Robert Chance

13. The stipulation signed by defense counsel and the prosecutor states that Robert Chance, if called to testify, would have testified that he is a chemist employed by NYPD's laboratory. That he received a degree in chemical engineering from University of Calicut, and has served as a chemist at the NYPD laboratory since April 2000. That Mr. Chance has performed in excess of 6,000 tests to determine the presence or absence of heroin or cocaine, and that the Court would have declared and accepted his testimony as that of an expert witness.

Summation

14. During the prosecutor's summation, the assistant district attorney held up the stipulation and the lab reports and told the jurors that "Mr. Chance would have testified to this if he were called to testify." Defense counsel waived appellant's right to

confront the analyst and failed to render a timely objection.

The Deliberation

15. After the Court's charge to the jury, the juror's were sent to the jury room to deliberate. Sometime thereafter, the jurors sent out a note. Prior to responding to the note, the Court brought the prosecutor, defense counsel, appellant, and all of the jurors into the courtroom. Without reading the note into the record or marking it as an exhibit the judge began to recite the elements of criminal possession of a controlled substance in the second degree to the jurors. No objection was rendered by trial counsel, and within 20 minutes after leaving the courtroom the jury returned with a verdict of guilty. T.T. 450-462.

Issues Raised By Appellate Counsel

POINT I

AN INDEPENDENT REVIEW OF THE RECORD REVEALS NO NONFRIVIOLOUS ISSUES THAT CAN BE RAISED ON APPEAL.

Inadequacy of Filed Brief

16. As previously set forth, the appeal herein was perfected by assigned counsel. The brief as submitted did not present well reasoned arguments to this Court. Firstly, the Anders brief filed by appellate counsel on behalf of appellant claimed that there were no nonfrivolous issues that could be raised on appeal, and appellate counsel asked to be relieved as counsel. See Anders v. California, 386 U.S. 738.

17. Further, the record reflects that the Court, in addressing the note sent out by the jurors during the deliberation process, did so in violation of appellant's right to due process of law.

18. Therefore, the argument advanced by appellate counsel that there were no nonfrivolous issues that can be raised on appeal "flies in the face of the record."

Meritorious Issues Ignored By Appellate Counsel

19. Assigned appellate counsel not only inadequately represented appellant on his direct appeal to this Court by basically

abandoning appellant's appeal, but also omitted meritorious arguments upon which a reversal of the conviction could have been obtained. These issues were supported by the facts in the record, statutory law, and prior decisional law. These arguments are obvious from even a casual reading of the record, but were ignored on appeal.

20. In the instant matter, the record reveals that upon receipt of the last note sent out by the jury, the trial Court brought the assistant district attorney, all of the jurors, defense counsel, and appellant into the courtroom. The jury note was not marked as an exhibit, the Court didn't read the note into the record, and the Court proceeded to recite the elements of criminal possession of a controlled substance in the second degree to the jurors. No objection was rendered by trial counsel, and within twenty (20) minutes after leaving the courtroom the jury returned with a verdict of guilty. T.T. 450-462.

21. Over fifteen years before appellate counsel was assigned to represent appellant on his direct appeal, the legislature enacted Criminal Procedure Law §310.30 which provides:

> "At any time during its deliberation, the jury may request the court for further instruction or information with respect to the law, with respect to the content or substance of any

trial evidence, or with respect to any other matter pertinent to the jury's consideration of the case. Upon such a request, the court must direct that the jury be returned to the courtroom and, after notice to both the people and counsel for the defendant, and in the presence of the defendant, must give such requested information or instruction as the court deems proper."

22. CPL §310.30 imposes two separate duties on the court following a substantive juror inquiry, i.e., the duty to notify counsel, and the duty to respond. The requirement that "notice" be given to counsel is not a mere formality or a procedural device designed only to ensure counsel's presence in the courtroom when the court gives its response to the jurors' request for information or instruction. See People v. Ramsey, 40 A.D.2d 837, 838; People v. Merrill, 286 A.D.2d 307.

23. While it is undoubtedly one of the statutes purposes, an equally important purpose is to ensure that counsel has the opportunity to be heard before the response is given. See Rogers v. United States, 422 U.S. 35, 39; United States v. Robinson, 560 F.2d 507, 516 (2d Cir.) [en banc], cert, denied, 435 U.S. 905.

24. As the Court of Appeals emphasized in People v. O'Rama, 78 N.Y.2d 270, 277 (1991), "the trial court's core responsibility under

the statute is both to give meaningful notice to counsel of the specific content of the jurors' request--in order to ensure counsel's opportunity to frame intelligent suggestions for the fairest and least prejudicial response--and to provide a meaningful response to the jury." The Court of Appeals then outlined the following procedure for dealing with jury notes:

> "[W]henever a substantive written jury communication is received by the Judge, it should be marked as a court exhibit and, before the jury is recalled to the courtroom, read into the record in the presence of counsel. Such a step would ensure a clear and complete record, thereby facilitating adequate and fair appellate review. After the contents of the inquiry are placed on the record, counsel should be afforded a full opportunity to suggest appropriate responses... [T]he trial court should ordinarily apprise counsel of the substance of the responsive instruction it intends to give so that counsel can seek whatever modifications are deemed appropriate before the jury is exposed to the potentially harmful information."

25. Although the Court of Appeals recognized that some departures from the procedures outlined in O'Rama may be subject

to the rules of preservation, a failure to fulfill the court's core responsibility in allowing appellant his right to the assistance of counsel is not. The court's error in failing to disclose the contents of the note had the effect of entirely preventing defense counsel from participating meaningfully in this critical stage of the trial and represented a significant departure from the "organization of the court of the mode of proceedings prescribed by law." This error also presented a question of law on appeal within the meaning of CPL §470.05(2), notwithstanding that trial counsel did not object to the court's procedure. See People v. Coons, 75 N.Y.2d 796, 797, quoting, People v. Patterson, 39 N.Y.2d 288, 295, aff'd, 432 U.S. 197.

26. This case is similar to the case of People v. Cook, 202 A.D.2d 443, where the Appellate Division for the Second Department ruled that "although the Trial Judge erred by refusing defense counsel the opportunity to suggest responses to the note from the juror, the error was harmless in light of the overwhelming evidence of defendant's guilt." In Cook, the victim was shot during a robbery of a delivery truck. There was an eyewitness to the crime, and a police officer who testified that the defendant admitted his involvement in the robbery. Despite the Second Department's ruling in Cook, the Court of Appeals agreed that the trial judge erred by refusing defense

counsel the opportunity to suggest responses to the note from the juror, but declined to agree that the error was harmless. In Cook, just as in O'Rama, the Court of Appeals held that the Court entirely deprived defendant of his right to have specific input into the court's response to the single juror's note. And that, moreover, just as in O'Rama, the court's response to the single juror's note "was unquestionably intended to have an effect on the deliberative process." The Court of Appeals concluded that the trial courts' denial of defendant's opportunity to participate in the charging decision was inherently prejudicial, reversed the conviction, and ordered a new trial. See People v. Cook, 85 N.Y.2d 928, 931, citing People v. O'Rama, supra, at 280.

27. At issue on this application is not whether appellate counsel's strategy could, with the benefit of hindsight been improved, the issue is rather one of basic competence. Here, appellate counsel had before him a trial record in which there was a "mode of proceedings error" that would have resulted in a reversal of appellant's conviction had appellate counsel raised this colorable claim on appeal. Yet, this substantive issue was not even raised, much less argued.

28. It is well settled that the unexplained failure of counsel to raise issues which, if raised, would have rendered a reversal or modification likely, constitutes a sufficient ground upon which to predicate a finding of

ineffective assistance of appellate counsel. That criterion has been amply satisfied in this case. Given the nature of the unbriefed issue, it was not merely likely, but virtually certain that had the relevant points been raised regarding the jurors' note, appellant's conviction would have been reversed. When there is added to this very basic failure of appellate representation, the evident lack of care and confusion which suffused the briefing of those issues counsel thought appropriate to raise, it becomes apparent that appellant has not merely presented a sufficient, but overwhelmingly meritorious claim of ineffective assistance of appellate counsel. This is a case in which counsel's failure to render competent representation palpably diminished the court's capacity to do justice. Indeed, unless the efforts of counsel are to be deemed irrelevant to the quality of our jurisprudence, it would seem that the within application must be granted.

29. Accordingly, the application for a writ of error coram nobis should be granted, the aforesaid Order of this Court should be recalled and vacated, and the judgment convicting appellant of criminal possession of a controlled substance in the second degree should be reversed and the matter remanded for a new trial. People v. Rutter, 202 A.D.2d 123; People v. Rodriguez, 185 A.D.2d 198; See Also Strickland v. Washington, 466 U.S. 668.

WHEREFORE, it is respectfully requested that an Order issue from this Court affirming the conviction of your deponent upon the grounds that he was deprived of the effective assistance of appellate counsel, and granting such other and further relief as the court may deem just and proper.

Respectfully submitted,

_____

_____ # _____
Petitioner Pro Se
_____ Correctional Facility

_____

_____ NY _____

Sworn to before me this
_____ day of _____ 20___.
_____

SUPREME COURT OF THE STATE OF NEW YORK COUNTY
OF _____
--X

The People of the State of New York
                              (SAMPLE)
    Plaintiffs,   **MEMORANDUM OF LAW**

    -against-   _____COUNTY
_____,

Defendant-Appellant.
                            IND NO._____
--X

PRELIMINARY STATEMENT

    This Memorandum of Law is submitted in support of appellant's motion for a writ of error coram nobis. The motion is based upon the ground that appellant was denied his state and federal right to the effective assistance of appellate counsel during his direct appeal to this Court from a judgment of conviction, entered in the Supreme Court, County of _____, for the crime of criminal possession of a controlled substance in the second degree.

STATEMENT OF FACTS

    The facts which provide the basis for the arguments contained within this Memorandum of Law have already been detailed in appellant's affidavit submitted herewith and in support of the instant motion. In the interest of brevity, appellant does not rewrite them here. Instead, appellant has incorporated those facts into this memorandum of law by reference, and re-alleges them as fully set forth in the affidavit.

ARGUMENT

GROUND I

APPELLANT HAS THE RIGHT TO CHALLENGE THE INEFFECTIVE ASSISTANCE OF APPELLATE COUNSEL.

Appellant has the right to challenge the ineffective assistance of appellate counsel collaterally by bringing a motion for a writ of error coram nobis in the appellate court where the ineffective assistance occurred. People v. Bachert, 69 N.Y.2d 593, 516 N.Y.S.2d 623 (1987). There is no time limit on the filing of collateral attacks on judgments of conviction. Cf. People v. Jackson, 78 N.Y.2d 638, 578 N.Y.S.2d 483 (1991). Appellant's appeal was heard and disposed of in the Appellate Division, Second Department. Therefore, this Court can properly hear appellant's challenge based on the ineffective assistance of his appellate attorney.

GROUND II

APPELLANT'S RIGHT TO THE EFFECTIVE ASSISTANCE OF COUNSEL ON HIS STATE COURT DIRECT APPEAL WAS VIOLATED WHEN

HIS ASSIGNED APPELLATE COUNSEL OMITTED SUBSTANTIAL AND OBVIOUS ISSUES WHILE PURSUING ISSUES THAT WERE CLEARLY AND SIGNIFICANTLY WEAKER.

It is well established that every state criminal defendant has a due process right to the effective assistance of counsel on direct appeal in a criminal case. See Evitts v. Lucey, 459 U.S. 387, 105 S.Ct. 830 (1985); See Also Strickland v. Washington, 466 U.S. 668, 104 S.Ct. 2052 (1984).

This requires appellate counsel to act as an advocate, not merely a amicus curiae, and to marshal legal arguments on appellant's behalf in order that he might have a full and fair resolution and consideration on his appeal. Anders v. California, 386 U.S. 738, 743-744, 87 S.Ct. 396 (1967); Douglas v. United States, 356 U.S. 674, 78 S.Ct. 974 (1958). This also requires that "he support his client's appeal to the best of his ability" (Anders v. California, supra at 744), and the brief he submits must reflect more than "a detached evaluation of the appellant's claim." See Evitts v. Lucey, supra at 394.

In order to prevail on a claim of ineffective assistance of appellate counsel under the federal standard, a two-part test must be satisfied. First, appellant "must show that his attorney's performance 'fell below an objective standard of reasonableness,' and second, he must show that there is a 'reasonable probability' that but for counsel's error, the outcome would have been different." Mayo v. Henderson, 13 F.3d 528, 533 (2d Cir.1994).

To satisfy the first part of the test, appellant must show that "appellate counsel omitted significant and obvious issues while pursuing issues that were clearly and significantly weaker." Id. at 533. This must be evaluated according to the facts of the case in conjunction with counsel's failure to present a particular claim as of the time of direct appeal, and hindsight to second guess his strategy may not be used.

"However, the omission of a meritorious claim cannot be excused simply because an intermediate appellate court would have rejected it." Id. at 533-534. In fact, the omission of a meritorious claim cannot be excused even when the claim was presented in a pro se supplemental brief and specifically rejected by the appellate court: "it is quite possible that an attorney would have found other arguments or would' have been more articulate in the representation of the case on appeal." Jenkins v. Coombe, 321 F.2d 158, 161 (2d Cir. 1987), cert, den., 484 U.S. 1008, 108 S.Ct. 704 (1988).

To satisfy the second part of the test (i.e., show a reasonable probability that the outcome of the direct appeal would have been different had counsel raised the omitted claim), appellate counsel's failure to present the particular claim in question must sufficiently "undermine confidence in the outcome" of the direct appeal. "This determination may be made with the benefit of hindsight." Mayo v. Henderson, supra, at 534.

In New York State it is well settled that "the unexplained failure of counsel to raise issues which, if raised, would have rendered a reversal or modification likely, constitutes a sufficient ground upon which to predicate a finding of ineffective assistance of appellate counsel." People v. Rodriguez, 185 A.D.2d 198; People v. Rutter, 202 A.D.2d 123.

Appellant's appellate counsel failed in his duty to present meritorious arguments on appellant's behalf during the direct appeal, even though, based upon the law in existence at the time of the direct appeal, he could have. As a result, appellate counsel did not afford appellant the quality of representation to which he was constitutionally entitled. While ignoring the meritorious issues, appellate counsel proceeded to raise issues that were clearly and significantly weaker.

The point raised by appellate counsel in the brief was, for the most part, a total abandonment of appellant's appeal. Assigned counsel completely failed in his duty to marshal arguments on defendant's behalf, and as a result, did not afford appellant the quality of representation to which he was constitutionally entitled. Most notably, appellate counsel did not raise a solidly meritorious argument regarding the trial court's denying appellant's trial counsel the right to have input into the court's response to a jury note. This argument, grounded in state and federal law at the time of appellant's direct appeal, would more than likely have won appellant a reversal on his appeal.

Prior to the appeal in this matter, it was well settled that "messages from a jury should be disclosed to counsel and that counsel should be afforded an opportunity to be heard before the Trial Judge responds." Rogers v. United States, 422 U.S. 35, 39, 95 S.Ct. 2091 (1975); People v. O'Rama, 78 N.Y.2d 270, 574 N.Y.S.2d 159 (1991).

The requirement that "notice" be given to counsel is not a mere formality or a procedural device designed only to ensure counsel's presence in the courtroom when the court gives its response to the juror's request for information or instruction. People v. Ramsey, 40 A.D.2d 837, 838, 337 N.Y.S.2d 332; People v. Merrill, 286 A.D.2d 307, 143 N.Y.S.2d 376.

While it is undoubtedly one of the statutes purposes, an equally important purpose is to ensure that counsel has the opportunity to be heard before the response is given. Rogers v. United States, 422 U.S. 35, 39, 95 S.Ct. 2091, 2094-2095; United States v. Robinson, 560 F.2d 507, 516 (2d Cir.) [en banc] cert. denied, 435 U.S. 905, 98 S.Ct. 1451.

Such an opportunity is essential to counsel's ability to represent the client's interests and, further to ensure the protection of the client's constitutional and statutory rights at these critical postsubmission proceedings. Thus, just as CPL §310.30's requirement that juror inquiries be answered mandates a "meaningful" response, so too does that statute's "notice" requirement mandate notice that is meaningful. People v. Ciaccio, 47 N.Y.2d 431, 436, 418 N.Y.S.2d 371.

This case is similar to the case of People v. Cook, 202 A.D.2d 443, wherein the Appellate Division for the Second Department ruled that "although the Trial Judge erred by refusing defense counsel the opportunity to suggest responses to the note from the juror, the error was harmless in light of the overwhelming evidence of defendant's guilt." In Cook, the victim was shot during a robbery of a delivery truck. There was an eyewitness to the crime, and a police officer who testified stated that the defendant admitted his involvement in the robbery. In Cook, just as in O'Rama, the Court of Appeals concluded that the trial court's denial of defendant's opportunity to participate in the charging decision was inherently prejudicial and reversed the conviction. People v. Cook, 85 N.Y.2d 928.

In the case of People v. Martin, the Appellate Division, Fourth Department, granted a defendant's motion for a writ of error coram nobis based on the contention of defendant that he was denied his right to effective assistance of appellate counsel because counsel failed to argue in the prior appeal "that the defense was never given an opportunity to review the various jury notes, or to have input into the trial court's response to such notes." People v. Martin, 26 A.D.3d 847.

The appeal of Martin's case was consolidated with that of People v. Kisoon, to determine whether a trial court committed a mode of proceedings error when it failed to disclose, or significantly paraphrased a jury note, the Court of Appeals in deciding the issue, concluded that it did. See People v. Kisoon, 8 N.Y.3d 129, 831 N.Y.S.2d 738.

"[T]here are few moments in a criminal trial more critical to its outcome than when the court responds to a deliberating jury's request for clarification of the law or further guidance on the process of deliberations. Indeed, the court's response may well determine whether a verdict will be reached, and what that verdict will be." People v. Kisoon, 8 N.Y.3d at 134-135.

After charging the jury on the elements of the crime, the jury returned with a verdict of guilty within twenty (20) minutes after leaving the courtroom. Clearly, in the instant matter, as in O'Rama, the "court's failure to notify counsel of the note's contents, which resulted in a denial of the right to participate in the charging decision, was inherently prejudicial." O'Rama, supra, 78 N.Y.2d at 280.

Although the Court of Appeals recognized that some departures from the procedures outlined in O'Rama may be subject to the rules of preservation, a failure to fulfill the court's core responsibility in allowing appellant his core right to the assistance of counsel is not. The court's error in failing to disclose the contents of the note had the effect of entirely preventing defense counsel from participating meaningfully in this critical stage of the trial represented a significant departure from the "organization of the court or the mode of proceedings prescribed by law." People v. Kisoon, 8 N.Y.3d 129.

Appellant strongly asserts that appellate counsel should have known that the court's failure to follow the dictates of CPL §310.30 was reversible error that was not subject to harmless error analysis, and also reviewable in spite of trial counsel's failure to object. Therefore, the criterion for ineffective assistance of appellate counsel has been amply satisfied in this case. Given the nature of the unbriefed issues, particularly those relating to the court's failure to notify appellant's trial counsel of the contents of the juror's note, it was not merely likely, but virtually certain, that had the relevant points been raised regarding the jury note, appellant's conviction would have been reversed. When there is added to this very basic failure of appellate representation, the evident lack of care and confusion which suffused the briefing of those issues that counsel thought appropriate to raise, it becomes apparent that appellant has not merely presented a sufficient, but an overwhelmingly meritorious claim of ineffective assistance of appellate counsel.

ACCORDINGLY, the unexplained failure of counsel to raise this issue which, if raised, would have rendered a reversal, constitutes sufficient ground upon which the within application for a writ of error coram nobis should be granted, and the judgment convicting appellant of criminal possession of a controlled substance in the second degree should be reversed and the matter remanded for a new trial. People v. Rutter, 202 A.D.2d 123; Strickland v. Washington, 466 U.S. 668; U.S. Const., 5th, 6th, and 14th Amends.; N.Y. Const., Art. I, §6.

Dated: _____, ____, 20__.
_____, New York

        Respectfully submitted,

_____ # _____
Petitioner Pro Se
_____ Correctional Facility

_____ NY _____

SUPREME COURT OF THE STATE OF NEW YORK
APPELLATE DIVISION: _____ DEPARTMENT
_____

THE PEOPLE OF THE STATE OF NEW YORK,
    Respondent,   _____ COUNTY
    -against-
_____ #_____, IND. NO. _____
    Defendant-Appellant
_____

(BLANK)
WRIT OF ERROR CORAM NOBIS
FOR
APPELLANT-PETITIONER

_____
APPELLANT PRO SE
_____Correctional Facility
_____
_____

SUPREME COURT OF THE STATE OF NEW YORK COUNTY
OF _____

--X

The People of the State of New York

        Plaintiffs,   **NOTICE OF MOTION FOR**
                                  WRIT OF ERROR CORAM
        -against-   **NOBIS**

_____,

Defendant-Appellant.

                              IND NO._____

--X

    PLEASE TAKE NOTICE, that upon the annexed affidavit of _____ sworn to on the _____ day of _____, 20____, and all the documents attached thereto, and upon the proceedings heretofore had herein, appellant will move this Court at a term thereof to be held at the Appellate Division, _____ Department Courthouse located at _____, on the _____ day of _____, 20____ at ten o'clock in the forenoon of that day, or as soon thereafter as counsel may be heard for an Order vacating the _____ _____, 20____, Decision and Order of this Court affirming his conviction, and granting such other and further relief as may be just and proper upon the ground that he was denied his right to the effective assistance of counsel under the Fifth, Sixth, and Fourteenth Amendments of the United States Constitution on his direct appeal to this Court because:

(a) the assistance provided by his appellate counsel was so nominal it amounted to the substantial equivalent of being assigned no counsel at all; and

(b) if the assistance of appellate counsel was something more than nominal, it still did not reach a level of performance sufficient to satisfy an objective standard of reasonableness, and there is a 'reasonable probability' that but for counsel's deficient performance, the outcome of the appeal would have been different.

PLEASE TAKE FURTHER NOTICE, this motion is in the nature of Error Coram Nobis, and the answering papers, if any, shall be filed with proof of service on the undersigned at least seven (7) days before the return date of this motion in accordance with the provisions of C.P.L.R. §2214. This motion is submitted on the papers and personal appearance in opposition to the motion is neither required nor permitted.

Dated: _____, ___, 20__.
_____, New York

Respectfully submitted,

_____
_____ # _____
Petitioner Pro Se
_____ Correctional Facility
_____
_____ NY _____

TO: _____
_____ County District Attorney
_____
_____, NY _____

SUPREME COURT OF THE STATE OF NEW YORK COUNTY
OF _____
--X

The People of the State of New York

        Plaintiffs,   **AFFIDAVIT IN SUPPORT**
                                  OF MOTION FOR A WRIT
        -against-   **OF ERROR CORAM NOBIS**

_____,

Defendant-Appellant.
                        IND NO._____
--X
STATE OF NEW YORK   )
)ss.:
COUNTY OF _____)

    _____, being duly sworn, deposes and says:

    1. I am the above named defendant-appellant, am 18 years of age or older, and am currently incarcerated in the _____

    2. I make this affidavit in support of the instant motion for a writ of error coram nobis to vacate the _____, _____, 20___ Decision and Order of this Court affirming my conviction in the above matter. The basis of this motion is that I was deprived of my right to the effective assistance of counsel under the 5th, 6th, and 14th Amendments of the United States Constitution, and Article I, §6 of the New

York State Constitution upon my direct appeal to this Court from a judgment of conviction entered against me in the Supreme Court, County of _____, on _____ _____, 20___ in that:

 (a) THE ASSISTANCE PROVIDED BY MY APPELLATE COUNSEL WAS SO NOMINAL IT AMOUNTED TO THE SUBSTANTIAL EQUIVALENT OF BEING ASSIGNED NO COUNSEL AT ALL; and

 (b) IF THE ASSISTANCE OF APPELLATE COUNSEL WAS SOMETHING MORE THAN NOMINAL, IT STILL DID NOT REACH A LEVEL OF PERFORMANCE SUFFICIENT TO SATISFY AN OBJECTIVE STANDARD OF REASONABLENESS, AND THERE IS A 'REASONABLE PROBABILITY' THAT BUT FOR COUNSEL'S DEFICIENT PERFORMANCE, THE OUTCOME OF MY DIRECT APPEAL WOULD HAVE BEEN DIFFERENT.

PROCEDURAL HISTORY

 3. I was charged by indictment _____ and convicted in Supreme Court, County of _____, before Honorable (_____) after a jury trial.

 4. On _____ _____, 20___ Judge _____ sentenced me to a(n) determinate/indeterminate term of _____.

 5. I filed a timely notice of appeal and poor person application, and this Court assigned (_____), Esq., to perfect the appeal on my behalf.

6. This Court affirmed my conviction in a published opinion dated _____ _____, 20___. See _____, _____N.Y.S.2d___. I then applied to the New York State Court of Appeals for leave to appeal from this Court's Order of Affirmance. That application was denied on _____ _____, 20___. See Exhibit "A".

7. No prior application has been made to any Court to review the adequacy of the representation I received upon my direct appeal to this Court.

FACTS

Accordingly, the application for a writ of error coram nobis should be granted, the aforesaid Order of this Court should be recalled and vacated, and the judgment convicting appellant of should be reversed and the matter remanded for a new trial. People v. Rutter, 202 A.D.2d 123; People v. Rodriguez, 185 A.D.2d 198; See Also Strickland v. Washington, 466 U.S. 668.

WHEREFORE, it is respectfully requested that an Order issue from this Court affirming the conviction of your deponent upon the grounds that he was deprived of the effective assistance of appellate counsel, and granting such other and further relief as the court may deem just and proper.

                  Respectfully submitted,

                  _____#_____
                  Petitioner Pro Se
                  _____ Correctional Facility

                  _____ NY _____

Sworn to before me this _____ day of _____ 20____.
_____

SUPREME COURT OF THE STATE OF NEW YORK
APPELLATE DIVISION: _____ DEPARTMENT
--X

The People of the State of New York

    Plaintiffs,   **MEMORANDUM OF LAW**
   -against-   _____COUNTY

_____,

   Defendant-Appellant.
                   IND NO._____
--X

PRELIMINARY STATEMENT

    This Memorandum of Law is submitted in support of appellant's motion for a writ of error coram nobis. The motion is based upon the ground that appellant was denied his state and federal right to the effective assistance of appellate counsel during his direct appeal to this Court from a judgment of conviction, entered in the Supreme Court, County of _____, for the crime(s) of _____.

STATEMENT OF FACTS

    The facts which provide the basis for the arguments contained within this Memorandum of Law have already been detailed in appellant's affidavit submitted herewith and in support of the instant motion. In the interest of brevity, appellant does not rewrite them here. Instead, appellant has incorporated those facts into this memorandum of law by reference, and re-alleges them as fully set forth in the affidavit.

ARGUMENT

GROUND I

APPELLANT HAS THE RIGHT TO CHALLENGE THE INEFFECTIVE ASSISTANCE OF APPELLATE COUNSEL.

Appellant has the right to challenge the ineffective assistance of appellate counsel collaterally by bringing a motion for a writ of error coram nobis in the appellate court where the ineffective assistance occurred. People v. Bachert, 69 N.Y.2d 593, 516 N.Y.S.2d 623 (1987). There is no time limit on the filing of collateral attacks on judgments of conviction. Cf. People v. Jackson, 78 N.Y.2d 638, 578 N.Y.S.2d 483 (1991). Appellant's appeal was heard and disposed of in the Appellate Division, _____ Department. Therefore, this Court can properly hear appellant's challenge based on the ineffective assistance of his appellate attorney.

GROUND II

APPELLANT'S RIGHT TO THE EFFECTIVE ASSISTANCE OF COUNSEL ON HIS STATE COURT DIRECT APPEAL WAS VIOLATED WHEN HIS ASSIGNED APPELLATE COUNSEL OMITTED

SUBSTANTIAL AND OBVIOUS ISSUES WHILE PURSUING ISSUES THAT WERE CLEARLY AND SIGNIFICANTLY WEAKER.

It is well established that every state criminal defendant has a due process right to the effective assistance of counsel on direct appeal in a criminal case. See Evitts v. Lucey, 469 U.S. 387, 105 S.Ct. 830 (1985); See Also Strickland v. Washington, 466 U.S. 668, 104 S.Ct. 2052 (1984).

This requires appellate counsel to act as an advocate, not merely a amicus curiae, and to marshal legal arguments on appellant's behalf in order that he might have a full and fair resolution and consideration on his appeal. Anders v. California, 386 U.S. 738, 743-744, 87 S.Ct. 396 (1967); Douglas v. United States, 356 U.S. 674, 78 S.Ct. 974 (1958). This also requires that "he support his client's appeal to the best of his ability" (Anders v. California, supra at 744), and the brief he submits must reflect more than "a detached evaluation of the appellant's claim." See Evitts v. Lucey, supra at 394.

In order to prevail on a claim of ineffective assistance of appellate counsel under the federal standard, a two-part test must be satisfied. First, appellant "must show that his attorney's performance 'fell below an objective standard of reasonableness,' and second, he must show that there is a 'reasonable probability' that but for counsel's error, the outcome would have been different." Mayo v. Henderson, 13 F.3d 528, 533 (2d Cir.1994).

To satisfy the first part of the test, appellant must show that "appellate counsel omitted significant and obvious issues while pursuing issues that were clearly and significantly weaker." Id. at 533. This must be evaluated according to the facts of the case in conjunction with counsel's failure to present a particular claim as of the time of direct appeal, and hindsight to second guess his strategy may not be used.

"However, the omission of a meritorious claim cannot be excused simply because an intermediate appellate court would have rejected it." Id. at 533-534. In fact, the omission of a meritorious claim cannot be excused even when the claim was presented in a pro se supplemental brief and specifically rejected by the appellate court: "it is quite possible that an attorney would have found other arguments or would have been more articulate in the representation of the case on appeal." Jenkins v. Coombe, 821 F.2d 158, 161 (2d Cir.1987), cert, den., 484 U.S. 1008, 108 S.Ct. 704 (1988).

To satisfy the second part of the test (i.e., show a reasonable probability that the outcome of the direct appeal would have been different had counsel raised the omitted claim), appellate counsel's failure to present the particular claim in question must sufficiently "undermine confidence in the outcome" of the direct appeal. "This determination may be made with the benefit of hindsight." Mayo v. Henderson, supra, at 534.

In New York State it is well settled that "the unexplained failure of counsel to raise issues which, if raised, would have rendered a reversal or modification likely, constitutes a sufficient ground upon which to predicate a finding of ineffective assistance of appellate counsel." People v. Rodriguez, 185 A.D.2d 198; People v. Rutter, 202 A.D.2d 123.

Appellant's appellate counsel failed in his duty to present meritorious arguments on appellant's behalf during the direct appeal, even though, based upon the law in existence at the time of the direct appeal, he could have. As a result, appellate counsel did not afford appellant the quality of representation to which he was constitutionally entitled. While ignoring the meritorious issues, appellate counsel proceeded to raise issues that were clearly and significantly weaker.

The point(s) raised by appellate counsel in the brief was, for the most part, a total abandonment of appellant's appeal. Assigned counsel completely failed in his duty to marshal arguments on defendant's behalf, and as a result, did not afford appellant the quality of representation to which he was constitutionally entitled. Most notably, appellate counsel did not raise a solidly meritorious argument regarding: _____

(USE ADDITIONAL PAPER IF NECESSARY)

ACCORDINGLY, the unexplained failure of counsel to raise this issue which, if raised, would have rendered a reversal, constitutes sufficient ground upon which the within application for a writ of error coram nobis should be granted, and the judgment convicting appellant of criminal possession of a controlled substance in the second degree should be reversed and the matter remanded for a new trial. People v. Rutter, 202 A.D.2d 123; Strickland v. Washington, 466 U.S. 668; U.S. Const., 5th, 6th, and 14th Amends.; N.Y. Const., Art. I, §6.

Dated: _____, ____, 20__.
_____, New York

Respectfully submitted,

_____
_____ # _____
Petitioner Pro Se
_____ Correctional Facility
_____
_____ NY _____

28 U.S.C. §2241 MOTIONS FOR HABEAS CORPUS RELIEF

On a federal level the U.S. Supreme Court, any Circuit Court Judge and/or District Court may grant habeas corpus relief to a prisoner in federal custody. For the purposes of Gorilla Lawfair and its aim to keep "LAW FAIR," we are using this motion to focus on a situation that potentially has thousands of prisoners languishing in prison unjustly. The Federal Bureau of Prisons [FBOP] has adopted a policy of refusing to honor a state court judge's sentence that is directed to run concurrently with a previously imposed federal sentence where the prisoner is sent to a state facility and the time has been credited to the state sentence. Their rationale for this treatment is rooted in 18 U.S.C. §3585(b) which provides that a prisoner under the custody of FBOP cannot receive prior time credit that was previously credited towards another state or federal sentence. As we have already pointed out in the Sample Letter to the FBOP, and in the Sample 28 U.S.C. §2241 Motion for Habeas Corpus relief, failure to notice such an error in not honoring a sentencing judge's oral sentence "would seriously affect the fairness, integrity, or public reputation of judicial proceedings." And in situations where prisoners do not have the resources or a working knowledge of the law that applies to their situation they will have no choice but to serve unnecessary time in prison when they should in fact be free! The Sample Motion to Set Aside the Sentence is another example of how the issue can be argued by a prisoner who was sentenced in New York. For those who are faced with this situation occurring in other jurisdictions, the same federal law applies to them when it comes to the "plain error" doctrine. An issue such as this affects the substantial rights of every prisoner subjected to it. It took a great deal of research to put this one together and we hope that it will be of great service to those in need of relief.

A 28 U.S.C. motion for a writ of habeas corpus will not extend to a prisoner unless:

(1) He or she is in custody under the authority of the United States, or committed for trial before a court of the United States; or

(2) Is in custody for an act or omission while pursuing an act of Congress, or a decree of a United States Court; or

(3) Is in custody in violation of the Constitution or laws of the United States; or

(4) He or she needs to be brought to Court to testify for trial; or

(5) He or she is a foreign citizen in custody for an act or omission which is affected by the law of nations.

No detainees in Guantanamo Bay, Cuba will be allowed to have a petition heard by any court, jurisdiction or judge that is filed on their behalf under §2241.

WHERE TO FILE A §2241 PETITION

A §2241 motion can be filed in the District Court or Circuit that has jurisdiction to entertain it based upon where the individual is imprisoned. If the motion is filed in the District Court or Circuit Court of Appeals the original copy must be filed with the court, a copy must be served upon the warden of the institution where the person is imprisoned, and a copy must be served upon the attorney general of that particular state. The U.S. Supreme Court has jurisdiction as well, however, the Supreme Court and Circuit Court can refuse to hear your motion and transfer it to the District Court of your jurisdiction for resolution.

If your application is made to the Supreme Court you will have forward the original papers to the Supreme Court and forward a copy to the warden of the facility where the individual is imprisoned, and a copy to the attorney general of the particular state.

WHAT TO FILE

(1) Cover letter to the court clerk explaining exactly what papers you are forwarding along with the motion being filed with the court.

(2) Original petition for a writ of habeas corpus which outlines the facts pertaining to your situation and your legal arguments as to why you think the individual is entitled to "immediate release" from prison. You should also include any exhibits you

have to support your petition as well. We have included a Sample petition for a writ of habeas corpus as an example arguing the issue of an individual in federal custody serving a consecutive sentence even though the state sentencing court directed that the state sentence run concurrently with the federal sentence.

(3) Poor person application, which is an application stating that the petitioner is indigent and unable to afford the costs and fees associated with filing the petition. These can be obtained by writing to the court clerk. The poor person application can be sworn to "under the penalty of perjury" made pursuant to 28 U.S.C. §1745. Once an individual receives poor person status they will not be required to file as many copies of the petition that they normally would have had to file. Check with the clerk of the appropriate court for their filing procedures.

(4) An original proof of service sent to the appropriate court clerk along with the cover letter indicating that copies of your papers have been served upon the other parties, i.e., warden and attorney general.

WHAT TO EXPECT AFTER YOU FILE

After your papers are filed the attorney general will be given time to respond to the petition. When they respond the petitioner can and should reply with what is called a Traverse. A Traverse is conceptually the same as what is called a Reply. What it basically does is allow the petitioner to deny the allegations advanced by the attorney general that are not conceded. Before a ruling is issued on the motion it will be assigned to a Magistrate Judge who will review the motion and make a recommendation in accordance with 28 U.S.C. §636(b)(1). The petitioner can thereafter object to whatever they disagree with in the magistrate's report.

The matter will eventually go before a judge who will render a decision in the case. If the petition is not successful a notice of appeal must be filed in the court within 30 days after the denial. Federal Rules of Appellate Procedure §4(a).

(SAMPLE LETTER)

_____#_____
_____
_____
_____

_____ _____, 20____.

Federal Bureau of Prisons
320 First St., NW
Washington, DC 20534

    Re: Case No. 3:96-00100
       <u>Sentence Computation</u>

Dear Federal Bureau of Prisons:
    I am forwarding this letter to respectfully request that it be reviewed and considered as an appeal to have my sentence computed in accordance with lawful procedure and controlling United States Supreme Court precedents. Also, to correct a "clear error of law," and to prevent an ongoing "manifest injustice."

Background

    In August of 1995, the deponent was indicted on federal charges of bank robbery and use of a firearm during a crime of violence, with all charges to be tried in the United States District Court for the Western District of Virginia. New York State authorities arrested deponent on August 14, 1996 on charges of criminal use of a firearm in the first degree, attempted murder in the second degree, assault with intent to cause serious injury with a weapon, and attempted robbery for charges occurring on May 20, 1996.

Federal authorities obtained deponent from New York State authorities on January 13, 1997 via a writ of habeas corpus ad prosequendum, and transported him back to Virginia for proceedings on the federal charges. Petitioner was sentenced on February 12, 1998 in the United States District Court for the Western District of Virginia to 60 months imprisonment for bank robbery, and 60 months consecutive on the firearm charge. After sentencing, petitioner was returned to state authorities on March 8, 1998 and the federal judgments were filed with state authorities as a detainer on April 26, 1998.

After accepting a plea to the state charges, the state court in New York conducted sentencing proceedings on March 31, 1998. During the sentencing proceedings defense counsel for petitioner stated: "I rely on the promise [of seven and a half to fifteen years], but I know it is a little more complicated, as usual, insofar as he is in federal prison right now, as well, I have the number of the case in which he is serving the federal time, 3:96-00100." See Sentencing Minutes annexed as Exhibit "A".

The Trial Judge then pronounced: "The sentence of the Court is, as promised, seven and a half to fifteen years, that sentence to run concurrent with the federal sentence as referred to as case No. 3:96-00100." Rather than commit petitioner to the custody of the federal authorities, the clerk of the court issued a warrant of commitment that departed from the judge's oral pronouncement of sentence and committed petitioner to the custody of the state authorities. See Exhibit "B".

Petitioner was committed to the custody of the New York State Department of Correctional Services, now Department of Corrections and Community Supervision [DOCCS] on April 22, 1998. After being incarcerated for a total period of 9 years, 5 months and 10 days, petitioner was taken into custody by the United States Marshals Service [USMS]. Sometime thereafter, the Bureau of Prisons [BOP] prepared a sentence computation for petitioner, incorrectly commencing the 120 month sentence he received on January 24, 2006 and crediting petitioner with only 39 days of the entire 9 years, 5 months and 10 days towards his prior custody credit. To date, petitioner has been unsuccessful in his attempts to have this "clear error of law" corrected. However, petitioner strongly asserts that it is necessary to revisit this matter on the basis of the clerk's issuance of a commitment that departed from the state trial judge's oral pronouncement of sentence which resulted in a manifest injustice and denial of due process to deponent.

ARGUMENT

GROUND I

PETITIONER IS BEING DENIED HIS CONSTITUTIONAL RIGHT TO DUE PROCESS BASED UPON A COMMITMENT ORDER THAT DEPARTED FROM THE SENTENCING JUDGE'S ORAL PRONOUNCEMENT OF SENTENCE (U.S. CONST. XIV AMEND.).

In the instant matter, the sentence imposed by the United States District Court for the Western District of Virginia was a total of 120 months, or 10 years. The sentence of the state court in New York is "seven and a half to fifteen years, that sentence to run concurrent with the federal sentence as referred to as case No. 3:96-00100." However, after the concurrent sentence was orally pronounced by the judge, the clerk of the court issued a commitment that departed from the sentence issued by the judge and committed petitioner to the custody of the New York State authorities rather than the federal authorities. This departure from the judge's sentence resulted in an unconstitutional increase to petitioner's sentence and deprived petitioner of due process of law. See U.S. Const. XIV Amendment.

"[T]he sentence imposed by a sentencing judge is controlling; it is this sentence that constitutes the court's judgment and authorizes custody of the defendant." Hill v. United States ex rel. Wampler, 298 U.S. 460 (1936).

The goal of protecting a defendant's due process rights where matters of commitment are concerned was displayed in the United States Supreme Court decision in Hill v. United States ex rel. Wampler. In Hill, the clerk of the court, pursuant to custom, added a condition to the defendant's sentence of eighteen months and a $5,000 fine, specifically, that the defendant was to remain in custody until the fine was paid. In holding that the clerk did not have the power to alter the sentence imposed by the court by way of a "warrant of commitment," Justice Cardozo opined that "the only sentence known to the law is the sentence or judgment entered upon the records of the court...until corrected in a direct proceeding, it says what it was meant to say, and this is by an irrebuttable presumption." The court in Hill, therefore excluded a "warrant of commitment" prepared by the clerk of the court. See Hill v. United States ex rel. Wampler, 298 U.S. at p. 464.

Under New York Law, since petitioner's New York sentence was to run concurrent with the remainder of the undischarged term for which he was still responsible under federal authority, and petitioner was not returned to the custody of the federal authorities until 6 years, 9 months and 2 days after his New York sentence was imposed, petitioner's New York sentence did not legally commence (begin to run) until he was received into federal custody on January 24, 2005. New York Penal Law §70.20[3] and 70.30[2-a] both provide that "[Where a person who is subject to an undischarged term of imprisonment imposed at a previous time by a court of another jurisdiction is sentenced to an additional term or terms of imprisonment by a court of this state, to run concurrently with such undischarged term, such additional term or terms shall be deemed to commence when the said person is returned to the custody of the appropriate official of such other jurisdiction where the undischarged term of imprisonment is being served." Clearly, the sentencing minutes indicate that petitioner's sentence was to commence under the custody of the federal authorities. Due to the clerk's error, petitioner was unlawfully given credit towards his state sentence, resulting in a "breakdown in the adversarial process," wherein he is being denied credit for time towards his federal sentence. Petitioner's detention after that in DOCCS was illegal and in violation of petitioner's right to due process of law. See Exhibits "C" and "D".

The holding of Hill applies to a case such as the one here, as Hill went on to articulate a broader holding: "The judgment of the court establishes a defendant's sentence, and that sentence may not be increased by an administrator's amendment." Here, as in Hill, the clearly established precedent supports petitioner's claim. See Also Greene v. United States, 358 U.S. 326, 329 (1959), quoting Hill's assertion that: "The only sentence known to the law is the sentence or judgment entered upon the records of the court."

Deponent's imprisonment is authorized not by the sentence as calculated by BOP as consecutive to NYSDOCCS, but by the judgment of the court. See Hill 298 U.S. at 465 ("The prisoner is detained, not by virtue of the warrant of commitment, but on account of the judgment and sentence"). See Also United States v. A. Abras Inc., 185 F.3d 26, 29 (2d Cir.1999) (holding that the written judgment of commitment is simply evidence of the oral sentence); United States v. Marquez, 506 F.2d 620, 622 (2d Cir.1974) (holding that the oral sentence constitutes the judgment of the court and it is that sentence that provides the authority for the execution of the sentence).

Thus, the issue presented is simply whether the petitioner, who is currently incarcerated, was denied his due process rights under the constitution of the United States by the administrative imposition, post-sentence, of an unlawful commitment to the custody of NYSDOCCS instead of federal authorities upon which he is now being held past his 120 month sentence. The answer is clearly Yes!

If as in Hill, an erroneous order of commitment prepared by the clerk of the court with the court's knowledge cannot alter the sentence imposed by the court, then here an erroneous order of commitment prepared by the clerk of the court without the court's knowledge cannot do it. "Only the judgment of a court, as expressed through the sentence imposed by a judge has the power to constrain a person's liberty." See Hill v. United States ex rel. Wampler, 298 U.S. at 464 ("In any collateral inquiry, a court will close its ears to the suggestion that the sentence entered in the minutes is something other than the authentic expression of the sentencing judge").

The provision in the commitment order that was added by the clerk that petitioner be committed to NYSDOCCS which was not orally pronounced by the judge conflicts with not only the Fourteenth Amendment, but the Supremacy Clause of the Federal Constitution as well. Deponent has served almost 16 years. 6 years more than required by federal authorities. Unless this "clear error of law" and "manifest injustice" is rectified, petitioner will have to serve twice the sentence imposed upon him by the United States District Court for the Western District of Virginia, or 240 months.

Accordingly, since petitioner was sentenced concurrently, and the action by the court clerk erroneously committing petitioner to NYSDOCCS violates his due process rights under the Constitution of the United States, the Federal Bureau of Prisons should view the erroneous commitment as void, adopt and apply Hill to petitioner's application, and allocate him with the time served unlawfully in state custody. Which concurrent re-calculation will mandate petitioner's immediate release from federal custody.

GROUND II

PLAIN ERROR OCCURRED RESULTING IN A FUNDAMENTAL MISCARRIAGE OF JUSTICE IN VIOLATION OF DEFENDANT'S CONSTITUTIONAL RIGHT TO DUE PROCESS OF LAW (U.S. CONST. XIV AMEND).

Notwithstanding the heavy burden that a defendant faces when alleging plain error in sentencing, the Bureau of Prisons should find that the clerk in the New York State sentencing Court plainly erred by issuing a commitment that departed from the sentencing judge's oral pronouncement of sentence.

When reviewing cases for plain error, the Court of Appeals for the Fourth Circuit has held that: "In reviewing for plain error, our initial inquiry is whether an error occurred." In Hill, the court ruled that "the provision in the commitment order that was inserted by the clerk, but was not orally pronounced by the judge was void." Here, under New York Penal Law §70.20[3] and §70.30[2-a], petitioner was supposed to be "returned to the appropriate official of such other jurisdiction," i.e., the federal authorities, in order for the sentence imposed upon him by the judge to legally commence. The provision in the commitment order that was added by the clerk, that petitioner be committed to NYSDOCCS was not part of the sentence orally pronounced by the sentencing court and constitutes error.

The second prong of the plain error doctrine is that "[N]ext, the error must be plain." United States v. Hastings, 134 F.3d at 239. For purposes of plain-error review, "[plain is synonymous with 'clear' or, equivalently, 'obvious.'" United States v. Olano, 507 U.S. at 734, 113 S.Ct. 1770. When contrasting the oral sentence imposed by the sentencing judge in New York State with the erroneous commitment order prepared by the clerk and the prevailing law, the error committed by the clerk is nothing other than 'plain.'

Third, petitioner "must establish that the error affected his substantial rights, i.e., that it was prejudicial. United States v. Hastings, 134 F.3d at 240. To demonstrate that the error was prejudicial, petitioner must show that "the error actually affected the outcome of the proceedings." Id.; accord, United States v. Dominguez-Benitez, 542 U.S. 74, 124 S.Ct. 2333, 2339 (2004) (explaining that if an error is not structural, "relief... is tied in some way to prejudicial effect, and the standard phrased as 'error that affects substantial rights,' used in Rule

52, has previously been taken to mean error with a prejudicial effect on the outcome of the judicial proceeding").

The substantial rights inquiry conducted under Rule 52(b) is the same as that conducted for harmless error under rule 52(a), with the important difference that the burden rests on the defendant, rather than the government to prove that the error affected substantial rights. See United States v. Olano, 507 U.S. 725, at 734-35, 113 S.Ct. 1770; United States v. Williams, 81 F.3d 1321, 1326 (4th Cir.1996) (noting that on plain error review, "the question whether a forfeited plain error was actually prejudicial is essentially the same as the question whether nonforfeited error was harmless--the difference being only in the party who has the burden on appeal to show the error's effect").

A prejudice inquiry is governed by the standard set forth in Kotteakos v. United States, 328 U.S. 750, 66 S.Ct. 1239 (1946); See Williams, 81 F.3d at 1326.

In Kotteakos, the Supreme Court admonished that in determining whether an error affected a defendant's substantial rights the question is not whether an error-free proceeding would have produced the same result: "[l]t is not the appellate court's function to determine guilt or innocence. Nor is it to speculate upon probable reconviction and decide according to how the speculation comes out. Appellate judges cannot escape such impressions. But they may not make them sole criteria for reversal or affirmance. Kotteakos, 328 U.S. at 763, 66 S.Ct. 1239 (citations omitted).

Rather, the reviewing court must consider "what effect the error had or reasonably may be taken to have had upon" the outcome of the proceedings. Id. at 764, 66 S.Ct. 1239. "[I]f one cannot say with fair assurance after pondering all that happened without stripping the erroneous action from the whole that the judgment was not substantially swayed by the error, it is impossible to conclude that substantial rights were not affected." Kotteakos v. United States, 328 U.S. at 765, 66 S.Ct. 1239.

The question under the third prong of the plain error analysis is thus whether petitioner has established that he was deprived of his constitutional right to due process by the issuance of an erroneous commitment by the clerk of the court which committed him to the custody of NYSDOCCS instead of federal authorities which subjects him to time that "was no longer than that to which he would otherwise be subject." United States v. Angle, 254 F.3d 514, 518 (4th Cir.2001).

Petitioner has made such a showing. As explained above, petitioner was sentenced to 120 months, has served almost 16 years, and will have to serve 240 months, or twice the sentence imposed unless this manifest injustice is corrected. Hill v. United States ex rel. Wampler, 298 U.S. 460.

Finally, it needs to be determined whether the provision in the commitment order that was inserted by the clerk, but was not orally pronounced by the judge should be voided. As the court held in Hastings, "[O]ur discretion is appropriately exercised only when failure to do so would result in a miscarriage of justice, such as when the defendant is actually innocent or the error seriously affects the fairness, integrity or public reputation of judicial proceedings." United States v. Hastings, 134 F.3d 235, 239 (4th Cir.1998).

In the case of Sullivan v. Louisiana, 508 U.S. 275, 279, 113 S.Ct. 2078, the Supreme Court held: "The inquiry...is not whether, in a [proceeding] that occurred without the error," the same result would have been reached, "but whether the [outcome of] this [proceeding] was surely unattributable to the error." In short, the proper focus is on what actually happened as a result of the error, not what might happen in a subsequent proceeding on remand.

It should be concluded that exercise of discretion is warranted here. As a result of plain and prejudicial Fourteenth Amendment error, petitioner was re-sentenced by the clerk's error to a term of imprisonment twice as long as the sentence authorized by the United States District Court for the Western District of Virginia. There is no doubt that failure to notice such an error would seriously affect the fairness, integrity, or public reputation of judicial proceedings. See United States v. Ford, 88 F.3d 1350, 1356 (4th Cir.1996) (noticing a plain, prejudicial sentencing error that would have caused the defendant to "serve a term of imprisonment three years longer than required by the sentencing guidelines").

In U.S. v. Booker, 436 F.3d 238, 245-46 (D.C.Cir.2006), the court reasoned "In the context of criminal sentencing, we have long recognized 'that the pronouncement of sentence constitutes the judgment of the court.'" Gilliam v. United States, 269 F.2d 770, 772 (D.C.Cir.1959).

Therefore, once the court pronounces a criminal sentence--which constitutes "a judgment" —the Court clerk has no lawful authority to supplement the sentence with a second one because the sentencing judge's oral pronouncement constitutes the judgment of the court, and because the sentencing judge may impose one and only one judgment, the written judgment form is a nullity to the extent it conflicts with the previously pronounced sentence. See U.S. v. Booker, at pp. 245-46, citing Hill v. United States ex rel. Wampler, 298 U.S. 460, 464-65, 56 S.Ct. 760.

CONCLUSION

Accordingly, since petitioner has shown that "plain error" has occurred, petitioner should be granted concurrent nunc pro tunc designation in compliance with the oral sentence imposed by Hon. _____, of the New York County Supreme Court. Which concurrent re-calculation will mandate petitioner's immediate release from federal custody. See Hill v. United States ex rel. Wampler, 298. U.S. 460 ("A warrant of commitment departing in matter of substance from the judgment back of it is void. Being void and not merely irregular, its nullity may be established upon a writ of habeas corpus. The prisoner is detained, not by virtue of the warrant of commitment, but on account of the judgment and sentence. If the judgment and sentence do not authorize his detention, no "mittimus" will avail to make detention lawful"); See Also U.S. Const. XIV Amend.

I declare under the penalty of perjury that the foregoing is true and correct.

Executed on:_____ _____, 20__

UNITED STATES DISTRICT COURT
_____ DISTRICT OF _____

_____
_____, #_____
             PETITIONER,
V.
_____, WARDEN
             RESPONDENT.
_____

(SAMPLE)
MEMORANDUM OF LAW
FOR
A WRIT OF HABEAS CORPUS

_____
PETITIONER PRO SE
_____ CORRECTIONAL FACILITY
_____
_____

UNITED STATES DISTRICT COURT
_____ DISTRICT OF _____
---X
_____, #_____

                               (SAMPLE)
    Petitioner,   **MEMORANDUM OF LAW**

    V.

                            Case No. 3:96-00100
_____, WARDEN,

    Respondent.
---X

    This action is being brought pro se as a petition for a writ of habeas corpus pursuant to 28 U.S.C. §2241. This petition respectfully requests that it be reviewed and considered as a request to have petitioner's sentence computed in accordance with controlling United States Supreme Court precedents and to correct a "clear error of law," and to prevent a "manifest injustice."

Background

    In August of 1995, the deponent was indicted on federal charges of bank robbery and use of a firearm during a crime of violence, with all charges to be tried in the United States District Court for the Western District of Virginia. New York State authorities arrested deponent on August 14, 1996 on charges of criminal use of a firearm in the first degree, attempted murder in the second degree, assault with intent to cause serious injury with a weapon, and attempted robbery for charges occurring on May 20, 1996.

Federal authorities obtained deponent from New York State authorities on January 13, 1997 via a writ of habeas corpus ad prosequendum, and transported him back to Virginia for proceedings on the federal charges. Petitioner was sentenced on February 12, 1998 in the United States District Court for the Western District of Virginia to 60 months imprisonment for bank robbery, and 60 months consecutive on the firearm charge. After sentencing, petitioner was returned to state authorities on March 1998 and the federal judgments were filed with state authorities as a detainer on April 26, 1998.

After accepting a plea to the state charges, the state court in New York conducted sentencing proceedings on March 31, 1998. During the sentencing proceedings defense counsel for petitioner stated: "I rely on the promise [of seven and a half to fifteen years], but I know it is a little more complicated, as usual, insofar as he is in federal prison right now, as well, I have the number of the case in which he is serving the federal time, 3:96-00100." See Sentencing Minutes annexed as Exhibit "A".

The Trial Judge then pronounced: "The sentence of the Court is, as promised, seven and a half to fifteen years, that sentence to run concurrent with the federal sentence as referred to as case No. 3:96-00100." Rather than commit petitioner to the custody of the federal authorities, the clerk of the court issued a warrant of commitment that departed from the judge's oral pronouncement of sentence and committed petitioner to the custody of the state authorities. See Exhibit "B".

Petitioner was committed to the custody of the New York State Department of Correctional Services, now Department of Corrections and Community Supervision [DOCCS] on April 22, 1998. After being incarcerated for a total period of 9 years, 5 months and 10 days, petitioner was taken into custody by the United States Marshals Service [USMS]. Sometime thereafter, the Bureau of Prisons [BOP] prepared a sentence computation for petitioner, incorrectly commencing the 120 month sentence he received on January 24, 2006 and crediting petitioner with only 39 days of the entire 9 years, 5 months and 10 days towards his prior custody credit. To date, petitioner has been unsuccessful in his attempts to have this "clear error of law" corrected. However, petitioner strongly asserts that it is necessary to revisit this matter on the basis of the clerk's issuance of a commitment that departed from the state trial judge's oral pronouncement of sentence which resulted in a manifest injustice and denial of due process to deponent.

ARGUMENT

POINT I

PETITIONER IS BEING DENIED HIS CONSTITUTIONAL RIGHT TO DUE PROCESS BASED UPON A COMMITMENT ORDER THAT DEPARTED FROM THE SENTENCING JUDGE'S ORAL PRONOUNCEMENT OF SENTENCE (U.S. CONST. XIV AMEND.).

In the instant matter, the sentence imposed by the United States District Court for the Western District of Virginia was a total of 120 months, or 10 years. The sentence of the state court in New York is "seven and a half to fifteen years, that sentence to run concurrent with the federal sentence as referred to as case No. 3:96-00100." However, after the concurrent sentence was orally pronounced by the judge, the clerk of the court issued a commitment that departed from the sentence issued by the judge and committed petitioner to the custody of the New York State authorities rather than the federal authorities. This departure from the judge's sentence resulted in an unconstitutional increase to petitioner's sentence and deprived petitioner of due process of law. See U.S. Const. XIV Amendment.

"[T]he sentence imposed by a sentencing judge is controlling; it is this sentence that constitutes the court's judgment and authorizes custody of the defendant." Hill v. United States ex rel. Wampler, 298 U.S. 460 (1936).

The goal of protecting a defendant's due process rights where matters of commitment are concerned was displayed in the United States Supreme Court decision in Hill v. United States ex rel. Wampler. In Hill, the clerk of the court, pursuant to custom, added a condition to the defendant's sentence of eighteen months and a $5,000 fine, specifically, that the defendant was to remain in custody until the fine was paid. In holding that the clerk did not have the power to alter the sentence imposed by the court by way of a "warrant of commitment," Justice Cardozo opined that "the only sentence known to the law is the sentence or judgment entered upon the records of the court... until corrected in a direct proceeding, it says what it was meant to say, and this is by an irrebuttable presumption." The court in Hill, therefore excluded a "warrant of commitment" prepared by the clerk of the court. See Hill v. United States ex rel. Wampler, 298 U.S. at p. 464.

Under New York Law, since petitioner's New York sentence was to run concurrent with the remainder of the undischarged term for which he was still responsible under federal authority, and petitioner was not returned to the custody of the federal authorities until 6 years, 9 months and 2 days after his New York sentence was imposed, petitioner's New York sentence did not legally commence (begin to run) until he was received into federal custody on January 24, 2006. New York Penal Law §70.20[3] and §70.30[2-a] both provide that "[W]here a person who is subject to an undischarged term of imprisonment imposed at a previous time by a court of another jurisdiction is sentenced to an additional term or terms of imprisonment by a court of this state, to run concurrently with such undischarged term, such additional term or terms shall be deemed to commence when the said person is returned to the custody of the appropriate official of such other jurisdiction where the undischarged term of imprisonment is being served." Clearly, the sentencing minutes indicate that petitioner's sentence was to commence under the custody of the federal authorities. Due to the clerk's error, petitioner was unlawfully given credit towards his state sentence, resulting in a "breakdown in the adversarial process," wherein he is being denied credit for time towards his federal sentence. Petitioner's detention after that in DOCCS was illegal and in violation of petitioner's right to due process of law.[6] See Exhibits "C" and "D".

---

[6] NYSDOCCS was without legal authority to do anything other than follow the terms outlined in the commitment even though it was erroneous, under well-established New York case law, "prison officials are conclusively bound by the contents of commitment papers accompanying a prisoner." Murray v. Goord, 1 N.Y.3d 29, 32 (2003).

The holding of Hill applies to a case such as the one here, as Hill went on to articulate a broader holding: "The judgment of the court establishes a defendant's sentence, and that sentence may not be increased by an administrator's amendment." Here, as in Hill, the clearly established precedent supports petitioner's claim. See Also Greene v. United States, 358 U.S. 326, 329 (1959), quoting Hill's assertion that: "The only sentence known to the law is the sentence or judgment entered upon the records of the court."

Deponent's imprisonment is authorized not by the sentence as calculated by BOP as consecutive to NYSDOCCS, but by the judgment of the court. See Hill 298 U.S. at 465 ("The prisoner is detained, not by virtue of the warrant of commitment, but on account of the judgment and sentence"). See Also United States v. A. Abras Inc., 185 F.3d 26, 29 (2d Cir.1999) (holding that the written judgment of commitment is simply evidence of the oral sentence); United States v. Marquez, 506 F.2d 620, 622 (2d Cir.1974) (holding that the oral sentence constitutes the judgment of the court and it is that sentence that provides the authority for the execution of the sentence).

Thus, the issue presented is simply whether the petitioner, who is currently incarcerated, was denied his due process rights under the constitution of the United States by the administrative imposition, post-sentence, of an unlawful commitment to the custody of NYSDOCCS instead of federal authorities upon which he is now being held past his 120 month sentence. The answer is clearly Yes!

If as in Hill, an erroneous order of commitment prepared by the clerk of the court with the court's knowledge cannot alter the sentence imposed by the court, then here an erroneous order of commitment prepared by the clerk of the court without the court's knowledge cannot do it. "Only the judgment of a court, as expressed through the sentence imposed by a judge has the power to constrain a person's liberty." See Hill v. United States ex rel. Wampler, 298 U.S. at 464 ("In any collateral inquiry, a court will close its ears to the suggestion that the sentence entered in the minutes is something other than the authentic expression of the sentencing judge").

The provision in the commitment order that was added by the clerk that petitioner be committed to NYSDOCCS which was not orally pronounced by the judge conflicts with not only the Fourteenth Amendment, but the Supremacy Clause of the Federal Constitution as well. Deponent has served almost 16 years. Six years more than required by federal authorities. Unless this "clear error of law" and "manifest injustice" is rectified, petitioner will have to serve twice the sentence imposed upon him by the United States District Court for the Western District of Virginia, or 240 months.

Accordingly, since petitioner was sentenced concurrently, and the action by the court clerk erroneously committing petitioner to NYSDOCCS violates his due process rights under the Constitution of the United States, the Federal Bureau of Prisons should view the erroneous commitment as void, adopt and apply Hill to petitioner's application, and allocate him with the time served unlawfully in state custody. Which concurrent re-calculation will mandate petitioner's immediate release from federal custody.

POINT II

PLAIN ERROR OCCURRED RESULTING IN A FUNDAMENTAL MISCARRIAGE OF JUSTICE IN VIOLATION OF DEFENDANT'S CONSTITUTIONAL RIGHT TO DUE PROCESS OF LAW (U.S. CONST. XIV AMEND).

Notwithstanding the heavy burden that a defendant faces when alleging plain error in sentencing, the Bureau of Prisons should find that the clerk in the New York State sentencing Court plainly erred by issuing a commitment that departed from the sentencing judge's oral pronouncement of sentence.

When reviewing cases for plain error, the Court of Appeals for the Fourth Circuit has held that: "In reviewing for plain error, our initial inquiry is whether an error occurred." In Hill, the court ruled that "the provision in the commitment order that was inserted by the clerk, but was not orally pronounced by the judge was void." Here, under New York Penal Law §70.20[3] and §70.30[2-a], petitioner was supposed to be "returned to the appropriate official of such other jurisdiction," i.e., the federal authorities, in order for the sentence imposed upon him by the judge to legally commence. The provision in the commitment order that was added by the clerk, that petitioner be committed to NYSDOCCS was not part of the sentence orally pronounced by the sentencing court and constitutes error.[7]

The second prong of the plain error doctrine is that "[N]ext, the error must be plain." United States v. Hastings, 134 F.3d at 239. For purposes of plain-error review, "[p]lain is synonymous with 'clear' or, equivalently, 'obvious.'" United States v. Olano, 507 U.S. at 734, 113 S.Ct. 1770. When contrasting the oral sentence imposed by the sentencing judge in New York State with the erroneous commitment order prepared by the clerk and the prevailing law, the error committed by the clerk is nothing other than 'plain.'

Third, petitioner "must establish that the error affected his substantial rights, i.e., that it was prejudicial. United States

---

[7] Petitioner is not being denied concurrent nunc pro tunc "prior time credit" based on the fact that NYSDOCCS officials were "conclusively bound" to follow the erroneous order of commitment. Murray v. Goord, 1 N.Y.3d 29, 32; Cf. 18 U.S.C. §3585(b).

v. Hastings, 134 F.3d at 240. To demonstrate that the error was prejudicial, petitioner must show that "the error actually affected the outcome of the proceedings." Id.; accord, United States v. Dominguez-Benitez, 542 U.S. 74, 124 S.Ct. 2333, 2339 (2004) (explaining that if an error is not structural, "relief... is tied in some way to prejudicial effect, and the standard phrased as 'error that affects substantial rights,' used in Rule 52, has previously been taken to mean error with a prejudicial effect on the outcome of the judicial proceeding").

The substantial rights inquiry conducted under Rule 52(b) is the same as that conducted for harmless error under rule 52(a), with the important difference that the burden rests on the defendant, rather than the government to prove that the error affected substantial rights. See United States v. Olano, 507 U.S. 725, at 734-35, 113 S.Ct. 1770; United States v. Williams, 81 F.3d 1321, 1326 (4th Cir.1996) (noting that on plain error review, "the question whether a forfeited plain error was actually prejudicial is essentially the same as the question whether nonforfeited error was harmless--the difference being only in the party who has the burden on appeal to show the error's effect").

A prejudice inquiry is governed by the standard set forth in Kotteakos v. United States, 328 U.S. 750, 66 S.Ct. 1239 (1946); See Williams, 81 F.3d at 1326.

In Kotteakos, the Supreme Court admonished that in determining whether an error affected a defendant's substantial rights the question is not whether an error-free proceeding would have produced the same result: "[I]t is not the appellate court's function to determine guilt or innocence. Nor is it to speculate upon probable reconviction and decide according to how the speculation comes out. Appellate judges cannot escape such impressions. But they may not make them sole criteria for reversal or affirmance. Kotteakos, 328 U.S. at 763, 66 S.Ct. 1239 (citations omitted).

Rather, the reviewing court must consider "what effect the error had or reasonably may be taken to have had upon" the outcome of the proceedings. Id. at 764, 66 S.Ct. 1239. "[I]f one cannot say with fair assurance after pondering all that happened without stripping the erroneous action from the whole that the judgment was not substantially swayed by the error, it is impossible to conclude that substantial rights were not affected." Kotteakos v. United States, 328 U.S. at 765, 66 S.Ct. 1239.

The question under the third prong of the plain error analysis is thus whether petitioner has established that he was deprived of his constitutional right to due process by the issuance of an erroneous commitment by the clerk of the court which committed him to the custody of NYSDOCCS instead of federal authorities which subjects him to time that "was no longer than that to which he would otherwise be subject." United States v. Angle, 254 F.3d 514, 518 (4th Cir. 2001).

Petitioner has made such a showing. As explained above, petitioner was sentenced to 120 months, has served almost 16 years, and will have to serve 240 months, or twice the sentence imposed unless this manifest injustice is corrected. Hill v. United States ex rel. Wampler, 298 U.S. 460.

Finally, it needs to be determined whether the provision in the commitment order that was inserted by the clerk, but was not orally pronounced by the judge should be voided. As the court held in Hastings, "[O]ur discretion is appropriately exercised only when failure to do so would result in a miscarriage of justice, such as when the defendant is actually innocent or the error seriously affects the fairness, integrity or public reputation of judicial proceedings." United States v. Hastings, 134 F.3d 235, 239 (4th Cir.1998).

In the case of Sullivan v. Louisiana, 508 U.S. 275, 279, 113 S.Ct. 2078, the Supreme Court held: "The inquiry... is not whether, in a [proceeding] that occurred without the error," the same result would have been reached, "but whether the [outcome of] this [proceeding] was surely unattributable to the error." In short, the proper focus is on what actually happened as a result of the error, not what might happen in a subsequent proceeding on remand.

It should be concluded that exercise of discretion is warranted here. As a result of plain and prejudicial Fourteenth Amendment error, petitioner was re-sentenced by the clerk's error to a term of imprisonment twice as long as the sentence authorized by the United States District Court for the Western District of Virginia. There is no doubt that failure to notice such an error would seriously affect the fairness, integrity, or public reputation of judicial proceedings. See United States v. Ford, 88 F.3d 1350, 1356 (4th Cir.1996) (noticing a plain, prejudicial sentencing error that would have caused the defendant to "serve a term of imprisonment three years longer than required by the sentencing guidelines").

In U.S. v. Booker, 436 F.3d 238, 245-46 (D.C.Cir.2006), the court reasoned "In the context of criminal sentencing, we have long recognized 'that the pronouncement of sentence constitutes the judgment of the court.'" Gilliam v. United States, 269 F.2d 770, 772 (D.C.Cir.1959).

Therefore, once the court pronounces a criminal sentence -- which constitutes "a judgment" -- the Court clerk has no lawful authority to supplement the sentence with a second one because the sentencing judge's oral pronouncement constitutes the judgment of the court, and because the sentencing judge may impose one and only one judgment, the written judgment form is a nullity to the extent it conflicts with the previously pronounced sentence. See U.S. v. Booker, at pp. 245-46, citing Hill v. United States ex rel. Wampler, 298 U.S. 460, 464-65, 56 S.Ct. 760.

CONCLUSION

Accordingly, since petitioner has shown that "plain error" has occurred, petitioner should be granted concurrent nunc pro tunc designation in compliance with the oral sentence imposed by Hon. _____, of the New York County Supreme Court. Which concurrent re-calculation will mandate petitioner's immediate release from federal custody. See Hill v. United States ex rel. Wampler, 298 U.S. 460 ("A warrant of commitment departing in matter of substance from the judgment back of it is void. Being void and not merely irregular, its nullity may be established upon a writ of habeas corpus. The prisoner is detained, not by virtue of the warrant of commitment, but on account of the judgment and sentence. If the judgment and sentence do not authorize his detention, no "mittimus" will avail to make detention lawful"); See Also U.S. Const. XIV Amend.

I declare under the penalty of perjury that the foregoing is true and correct.

Executed on:_____ _____, 20___

_____
_____
Petitioner Pro Se
_____
_____
_____

PAROLE

Penal Law §1.05 - General Purposes:

"To insure the public safety by preventing the commission of offenses through the deterrent influence of the sentences authorized, the rehabilitation of those convicted, the promotion of their successful and productive reentry and reintegration into society, and their confinement when required in the interests of public protection."

Parole Defined

According to the Jailhouse Lawyer's Manual, parole is defined as "a system of discretionary release for prisoners who have not yet served their maximum sentences. Parole also refers to the process of your supervised reintegration into the community while you serve the remainder of your sentence outside of prison." In New York, the Division of Parole was established as part of the Executive Department on July 1, 1930. In 1967, legislation was passed which gave the Board of Parole the authority to "grant conditional release on parole to persons under definite sentences and to persons incarcerated in local reformatories."

Parole and Corrections

On January 1, 1971, the Division of Parole merged with the Department of Corrections and became the New York State Department of Correctional Services. Parole and Corrections merged based on the notion that a combined effort of penal institution and community supervision of convicted offenders would be a better way to deal with the reduction of crime through rehabilitation. After the passage of the Parole Reform Act in 1977, the Division of Parole once again became a separate part of the Executive Department on January 1, 1978. The legislation making Parole a separate entity apart from Corrections mandated that Parole establish Parole Guidelines regarding the minimum period of imprisonment (MPI) and their decisions to grant or deny parole release. The Parole Guidelines were eventually codified into the Executive Law. The Division of Parole also became responsible for the granting or denying of release to juveniles, and for community supervision on parole after release.

Parole Law Changes

During the 2010-2011 Budget, legislation was passed merging the Department of Corrections and the Division of Parole and changing their combined name to that of the Department of Corrections and Community Supervision. In addition to that, legislation was also enacted to reform the decision-making guidelines that seemed to have focused primarily on the nature of the crime and the person's criminal history. The 2011 amendments repealed §259-i(1) of the Executive Law that outlined the procedures for the Parole Board's setting of the minimum periods of imprisonment. Since 1980 the courts carried out this function anyway so it was of no effect where Parole Board action was concerned.

One of the significant changes to the Executive Law that went into effect on March 31, 2011 was to Executive Law §259-i(2)(c)(a) which reads:

> "Discretionary release on parole shall not be granted merely as a reward for good conduct or efficient performance of duties while confined but after considering if there is a reasonable probability that, if such inmate is released he will live and remain at liberty without violating the law, and that his release is not incompatible with the welfare of society and will not so deprecate the seriousness of his crime as to undermine respect for the law. In making the parole release decision the procedures adopted pursuant to subdivision four

of section two hundred fifty-nine (c) of this article shall require that the following be considered":

(i) "The institutional record including program goals and accomplishments, academic achievements, vocational education, training or work assignments, therapy and interactions with staff and inmates;
(ii) Performance if any, as a participant in a temporary release program;
(iii) Release plans including community resources, employment, education and training and support services available to the inmate;
(iv) Any deportation order issued by the federal government against the inmate while in custody of the department pursuant to section one hundred and forty-seven of the Correction Law;
(v) Any statement made to the Board by the crime victim or the victim's representative, where the crime victim is deceased or mentally or physically incapacitated;
(vi) The length of the determinate sentence to which the inmate would be subject had he or she received a sentence pursuant to section 70.70 or section 70.71 of the penal

law for a felony defined in article two hundred twenty or article two hundred twenty-one of the penal law;

(vii) The seriousness of the offense with due consideration to the type of sentence, length of sentence and recommendations of the sentencing court, the district attorney, the attorney for the inmate, the pre-sentencing probation report as well as consideration of any mitigating or aggravating factors, and activities following arrest prior to confinement; and

(viii) Prior criminal record, including the nature and pattern of the offenses, adjustment to any previous probation or parole supervision and institutional confinement."

The other significant amendment that became effective on October 1, 2011 regarding Parole Board decisions was that of Executive Law §259-c(4) which provides that the Board of Parole shall:

"Establish written procedures for its use in making Parole Board decisions as required by law. Such written procedures shall incorporate risk and needs principles to measure the rehabilitation of persons appearing before the Board, the likelihood of success of such persons upon release and assist members of the state Board of Parole in determining which inmates may be released to parole supervision."

Parole Memo

On October 5, 2011 which was only five days after the effective date of the statute, Andrea Evans, the Chairwoman of the Department of Community Supervision forwarded a memorandum regarding the new changes that provided in part:

> "As you know, members of the Board have been working with staff of the Department of Corrections and Community Supervision in the development of a transitional accountability plan (TAP). This instrument which incorporates risk and needs principles, will provide a meaningful measurement of an inmate's rehabilitation. With respect to the practices of the Boards, the TAP instrument will replace the inmate status report that you have utilized in the past when assessing the appropriateness of an inmate's release to parole supervision. To this end, members of the Board were afforded training in July 2011, in the use of a TAP instrument where it exists. Accordingly, as we proceed, when

staff have prepared a TAP instrument for a parole eligible inmate you are to use that document when making your parole release decisions... It is also important to note that the Board was afforded training in September 2011, in the usage of a COMPAS Risk and Needs Assessment tool to understand the interplay between that instrument and the TAP instrument, as well as understanding what each risk levels mean...

Therefore, in your consideration of the statutory criteria set forth in Executive Law §259-(i)(2)(c)(a)(i) through (viii) you must ascertain what steps an inmate has taken toward their rehabilitation and the likelihood of their success once released to parole release supervision. In this regard any steps taken by an inmate toward effecting their proposed release plans are to be discussed with the inmate during the course of their interview and considered in their deliberations."

Transitional Accountability Plan

The Transitional Accountability Plan (TAP) instrument was codified into Correction Law §71-a and reads, in part, as follows:

"Upon admission of an inmate committed to the custody of the department under an indeterminate or determinate sentence of imprisonment, the department shall develop a transitional accountability plan. Such plan shall be a comprehensive, dynamic and individualized case management plan based on the programming and treatment needs of the inmate. The purpose of such plan shall be to promote the rehabilitation of the inmate and their successful and productive reentry and reintegration into society upon release. To that end, such plan shall be used to prioritize programming and treatment services for the inmate during incarceration and any period of community supervision."

Assembly Corrections Committee

On November 20, 2011, the Assembly Corrections Committee held hearings regarding the new DOCCS agency. In attendance were Corrections Commissioner Brian Fischer, Community Supervision Chairwoman Andrea Evans, Assemblyman Jeffrion Aubry and others. When questioned by Assemblyman Aubry concerning the transitional accountability plan, Commissioner Fischer stated that:

"TAP will be in on July 1st... When TAP is ready to go, a Parole Board member can actually see the TAP, which would show from the beginning to end the entire progress... It will be ready this summer...COMPAS will be used to assign risk and--because it is a risk and needs assessment it's designed basically to create a mechanism by which we can assign risk levels to caseloads....The caseloads under COMPAS will be basically on four levels, very similar to that which we can assign risk levels to caseloads The caseloads under COMPAS will be basically on four levels, very similar to that which is already existing for using the TCJS risk needs assessment.... intensive supervision at 25 to 1... med-high supervision at 40-1... Regular supervision 80 to 1... low risk at 160 to 1. I believe, -- coming this January everybody coming out of prison will have a COMPAS done. And based on that the assignments will be made and the Parole Board will have access to it before they make their decisions."

COMPAS

COMPAS (Correctional Offender Management Profiling for Alternative Sanction) is an assessment tool designed by the Northpointe Institute for Public Management. COMPAS utilizes a questionnaire that is designed to assess three risks, i.e., "the risk of felony violence, the risk of re-arrest and the risk of absconding while under parole supervision." The April 20, 2012 New York Law Journal cited the Department of Corrections and Community Supervision as stating that the parole board panel were trained in the use of the risk assessment in 2011, and will undergo "intensive training" on June 22, 2012 regarding the COMPAS instrument.

Professor Phillip M. Genty

Professor Phillip M. Genty of Columbia University submitted an article to the New York Law Journal dated September 1, 2011, entitled "Changes to Parole Laws Signal Potentially Sweeping Policy Shift." In his article Professor Genty commented:

> "The 2011 amendments... modernize the work of the Parole Board by requiring the board to adopt procedures that incorporate a growing body of social science research about assessing post-release needs and recidivism risks.
>
> [T]he most important change is the replacement of static, past focused 'guidelines' with more dynamic present and future-focused risk assessment 'procedures' to guide the Parole Board...This addition of an explicit requirement that the Parole Board adopt and be guided by procedures that require it to evaluate rehabilitation'

and the likelihood of success... upon release signals a critical reform and modernization of parole practices. Such procedures... will rationalize parole decision-making by placing the focus primarily on who the person appearing before the Parole Board is today and on whether that person can succeed in the community after release, rather than - as under the previous 'guidelines' -- on who the person was many years earlier when he or she committed the crime. This is a shift of potentially sweeping significance."

The Thwaites Case
On December 21, 2011, Orange County Supreme Court Judge Lawrence H. Ecker issued the decision in the case of Matter of Thwaites v. New York State Bd. of Parole (N.Y.Slip Op.21453). The decision stemmed from a motion pursuant to CPLR Article 78 that was filed by Mr. Thwaites challenging the New York State Board of Parole's denying him release to parole supervision. Mr. Thwaites was sentenced to a term of 25 years to life for his convictions for murder 2° and assault 2°. Justice Ecker ruled that Mr. Thwaites should be given a new hearing before a different panel of the parole board because (1) "the Board's decision was not made in accordance with the 2011 Amendments to the Executive Law which requires a new

parole hearing utilizing risk assessment principles and procedures"; and (2) "[T]he Parole Board's determination also failed to indicate whether consideration was given to whether release to the deportation order with mandatory removal was appropriate under the circumstances of this case."

Although Mr. Thwaites appeared before the Parole Board on March 16, 2010 and the amendments to the Executive Law weren't effectuated until 2011, Justice Ecker concluded that the amendments were remedial and "should be given retroactive effect in order to effectuate its beneficial purpose." Therefore, anyone who appeared before the Parole Board before the effective date of the changes should raise the argument. Also, since the Commissioner of Corrections has stated that the Board wouldn't be trained in the use of the COMPAS instrument until July 1, 2012, it provides an argument for anyone denied parole release up to that point that the Parole Board didn't follow the mandatory guidelines prescribed by law.

Directive #4803

Directive #4803, dated March 16, 2012, illustrates the direction that the Department of Corrections and Community Supervision is striving to head towards in theory. It's Philosophy is that "[P]rograms are designed to promote the rehabilitation of the offender and their successful and productive reintegration into society." The directive establishes the guidelines for assigning programs to incarcerated individuals who are now referred to as "offenders." It also changed the title of counselors to "Offender Rehabilitation Coordinators." The directive outlines the procedures to be followed in order to provide offenders appropriate programming needs. It is also a change that is in compliance with the rehabilitative component of parole.

PREPARING FOR THE PAROLE BOARD

Usually, when a person is denied parole release the parole board utilizes some of the same language that it uses in just about every denial:

"YOUR CRIMINAL HISTORY IS EXTENSIVE."
"NATURE OF THE CRIME/INSTANT OFFENSE."
"YOU WILL NOT LIVE AND REMAIN AT LIBERTY WITHOUT VIOLATING THE LAW."
"YOUR RELEASE WILL UNDERMINE RESPECT FOR THE LAW."
"YOUR RELEASE IS NOT COMPATIBLE WITH THE WELFARE OF SOCIETY."
"CONSIDERATION HAS BEEN GIVEN TO AN ASSESSMENT OF YOUR RISKS AND NEEDS FOR YOUR SUCCESS ON PAROLE."

The new amendments to the Executive Law are designed to give the Board something to look at other than the seriousness of the offense and the person's prior criminal history which were the primary focus of the old guidelines. Andrea Evans, Chairwoman of the Division of Parole issued a memo dated October 5, 2011 wherein she referenced Executive Law §259-i(2)(c)(A) and stated:

"As noted by the New York State Court of Appeals in Silmon v. Travis, 95 N.Y.2d 470 (2000), the above-stated criteria reflect the strong rehabilitative component of section 259-i of the Executive Law.

Therefore, in your consideration of the statutory criteria set forth in Executive Law §259-i(2)(c)(A)(i) through (viii), you must ascertain what steps an inmate has taken toward their rehabilitation and the likelihood of their success once released to parole supervision. In this regard, any steps taken by an inmate toward effecting their rehabilitation, in addition to all aspects of their proposed release plan, are to be discussed with the inmate during the course of their interview and considered in your deliberations."

In order to properly prepare for the parole board an incarcerated individual should first do what is necessary for their rehabilitation. This is viewed as meeting your needs where appropriate programming is concerned and the various corrections and parole departments take this into consideration when making their assessments of individuals to determine whether or not they should be released to parole supervision. An individual's disciplinary history is also taken into account for release consideration. Therefore, it would be in an offenders best interests to do what they have to do to stay out of trouble and complete the necessary programming to enhance their chances of release.

COMPAS RE-ENTRY ASSESSMENT

The COMPAS (Correctional Offender Management Profiling for Alternative Sanction) Re-entry Assessment will take into consideration a person's:

- **Current Offenses-** also whether the person was on probation or under parole supervision at the time the crime occurred?
- **Criminal History-** how many prior criminal/juvenile offenses has the person had before, with special attention paid to violent acts.
- **Disciplinary History-** how many incidents of misbehavior has the person had within the past 24 months, with special attention paid to sexual misconduct, violence and drugs.
- **Classification History-** whether the person has been re-classified to a higher level for security reasons.
- **Family/Social Support-** has the person had family support during their incarceration and is continued family support anticipated upon their release?
- **Substance Use-** does the person have a substance abuse background and are they a risk for having future substance abuse problems?

- **Education-** has the person obtained a high school diploma or a G.E.D.? Do they have basic educational needs that need to be addressed?
- **Work and Financial-** does the person have job skills, current plans for employment or job offers (letters of reasonable assurance)?; does the person face employability and/or financial problems upon release?; does the person feel they need more training?; how does the person rate their own chance of being successful?

There are several factors that come into play with the COMPAS Re-entry Assessment. These factors along with the mandatory factors embodied in the Executive Law go hand in hand with the new "risk assessment" which includes "risk and needs" principles to measure the "rehabilitation" of persons appearing before the parole board, and "the likelihood of success of such persons upon release." Parole boards are entrusted with the duty of insuring public safety through the continued confinement of persons convicted of offenses "when required in the interests of public protection." N.Y. Penal Law §1.05. Therefore, it is up to you to convince them that you are ready to become a productive member of society should they release you to parole supervision.

Risk and Needs Assessment

The enactment of Chapter 62 of the laws of 2011, Part C, subpart A, §38-b, amended Executive Law §259-c(4) to mandate that the Parole Board shall:

> "establish written procedures for its use in making parole decisions as required by law. Such written procedures shall incorporate risk and needs principles to measure the rehabilitation of persons appearing before the board, the likelihood of success of such persons upon release and assist members of the state board of parole in determining which inmates may be released to parole supervision."

Risk is "the uncertainty of a result, happening or loss." Need is defined as "the lack of something important; a requirement; indigence." Parole commissioners have to weigh the uncertainty of a person re-offending should they decide to grant them release to community supervision. Uncertainty will always be a component because no one can predict the future. This is where the "needs" aspect comes into play. What qualities does the person appearing before the board lack or possess that can only serve to increase or decrease their chance of success upon release? Do you have a basic education? Do you have marketable job skills? Do you have a history of substance use? Have you prepared a relapse prevention plan? Do you have family/community support? Have you received any tickets in the past 24 months? Do you present a potential risk to public safety? Will your needs be met if you are released to parole supervision? Have you shown remorse for your victim(s)? Do you have insight into your criminal behavior? Have you taken responsibility for your actions? What are your re-entry plans (if any)?

    The above questions are key questions that an individual expecting to appear before the parole board must ask themselves and begin to seriously work on in the areas where they are lacking. Take a personal inventory of yourself that includes a "risk and needs assessment" in order that you may realistically measure your own rehabilitation and the likelihood of your success upon release. This way, when you do appear before the parole board it will make it a lot easier for them to get an idea of who the person sitting before them today is as opposed to the person you were when you committed the crime.

Crime Victims

    When you appear before the parole board they will ask you at some point if you have anything you would like to say. At that point it is up to you to represent on your own behalf. You should always have something to say, however, you should always begin and end your dialogue with emphasis placed on the remorse and empathy you have for your victim(s). It is not about you when you appear before the parole board. It is about your victim(s). Some individuals feel that they have a victimless crime because they either possessed or sold drugs. That way of thinking is unrealistic. How many people were robbed by individuals seeking to feed their drug habits? How many children went hungry at night because their parents used whatever money they had to purchase drugs rather than food? There is no such thing as a victimless crime. When crimes are committed it goes against the norms of society and under the law society is a victim of every crime committed. This is why the title of the cases in New York begin with "The People of the State of New York v." whoever the suspect is and federal cases begin with "United States v." whoever the suspect is.

Parole Packages

Parole packages are a way of presenting yourself to the board with the hope that they will read into it and see something that may convince them to decide to release you. There are many different styles that are utilized when putting them together, however, they should at least include the following information:

- Introduction
- Rap Sheet
- Presentence Investigation (PSI) Report

- Plea Minutes (if you copped out)
- Sentencing Minutes
- Inmate Status Report (If you have one)
- Personal Statement

In your personal statement you should cover the areas of remorse, responsibility, rehabilitation and redemption. When you cover those areas you should work on your re-entry plan as the conclusion of your parole package. Re-entry plans include your future plans, residence, employment and readiness. You should also include:

- Letters of Support (Family & Friends)
- Letters of Reasonable Assurance
- Community Petitions
- Relapse Prevention Plan
- Spirituality (Religion/Spiritual Practices)

A good resource for organizations that provide services and letters of reasonable assurance to incarcerated and formerly incarcerated individuals in New York State is Connections which is published every year by Correctional Library Services, The New York Public Library, 455 Fifth Avenue, New York, NY 10016. Connections is free of charge to incarcerated and formerly incarcerated people throughout New York State, as well as to staff members of agencies and others who provide them services.

The Jailhouse Lawyer's Manual is suggested reading for anyone looking to learn more about parole. Our main concern here is to get the information out about the new changes to the parole laws in New York State and what individuals can do according to these laws to enhance their chances of being released to parole supervision. The principles, however, apply to all states. The Jailhouse Lawyers Manual can be ordered by contacting Columbia Human Rights Law Review, 435 W. 115th St., New York, NY, 10027.

APPEALING FINAL PAROLE BOARD DECISIONS

The law governing administrative appeals of parole board decisions can be found in New York Executive Law §259-1(4). If you appeared before the parole board and a final decision issued denying you release on parole or you are assisting someone with appealing an unfavorable decision, a notice of appeal must be first filed within 30 days. The Notice of Appeal is usually sent along with the decision denying parole. When filling out the form make sure that it is indicated on the form that you wish to request a copy of the Hearing Transcript. The perfected appeal can be in the form of a letter or in the form of a Brief. We have provided a Brief of a Sample Appeal outlining some of the issues that could be raised on appeal and to show you the format of a brief. These issues, however, are not dispositive of the numerous issues that might be raised in an appeal. Whichever form you choose you must send four copies of your perfected appeal outlining your issues with any relevant documents in support and whatever portions of the Hearing Transcript that might be pertinent to your argument. Your Notice of Appeal and perfected appeal must be sent to:

New York State Board of Parole
Appeals Unit
1220 Washington Avenue
Albany, NY 12226

Once the Notice of Appeal is received, the Appeals Unit will forward a letter acknowledging their receipt of it. After they have transcribed the minutes they will send them along with a bill. Individuals appealing parole board decisions can also apply to the local court for counsel to aid them in the perfection of an appeal. Once counsel is applied for the appeals unit usually forwards the transcript of the hearing to the attorney.

After the appeal is perfected and filed with the appeals unit they have 120 days to render a decision. Once the 120 days have passed from the date your papers were filed you have exhausted your remedies and can now file an Article 78 Petition regarding your issues in court. The appeals unit almost never answers an appeal within the 120 day limit, however, they have been getting better with their responses as of late. You should work on putting together an Article 78 motion as soon as your appeal is sent to the appeals unit. This will give you plenty of time to conduct your research and prepare for the next phase of potential litigation. If you are successful in court you will only be entitled to a new board appearance, unless of course, if you have passed your conditional release date. We have included a Sample Article 78 Petition arguing issues pertaining to a final decision of the Parole Board to give you the format and see how they are put together. If you are capable and qualified to do it on your own it would consume less time. It takes about two months to obtain counsel. Once counsel is assigned they have to become familiarized with you and your hearing. By that time you could have already filed a perfected appeal on your own behalf and be waiting for the 120 day deadline to pass. Assigned lawyers do not usually help individuals with their Article 78 petitions who obtain poor person status because they only receive payment for the administrative appeal. There are some rare instances where lawyers will submit the Article 78 "pro bono" (for free). Prisoners are also entitled to a copy of their presentence report to prepare for their parole board appearance since it is one of the factors that the parole board must consider in determining whether the individual should be released or not. Prisoners are also entitled to a copy to prepare for their parole appeals. In Volume II of Gorilla Lawfair we have included motions for requesting a copy of the presentence report before or after a parole board appearance.

STATE OF NEW YORK
EXECUTIVE DEPARTMENT: DIVISION OF PAROLE
_____

In the Matter of the NEW YORK STATE
DIVISION OF PAROLE

    concerning

_____ # _____
NYSID # _____

****
(SAMPLE)
AN ADMINISTRATIVE PAROLE APPEAL
FROM A DENIAL OF PAROLE RELEASE
****

Mr. _____ # _____
Gowanda Correctional Facility
PO Box 311
Gowanda, NY 14070

STATEMENT OF RULING CHALLENGED

The Parole Board's decision was arbitrary, capricious and failed to satisfy the statutory requirements for parole release consideration.

NATURE OF THE CASE AND FACTS

This is an administrative appeal brought pursuant to Article 12-B of the <u>Executive Law</u>, §259-i(4) from a parole release hearing determination. Mr. _____ was originally received for his conviction for Manslaughter 2nd and Vehicular Assault 3rd. The sentence in this conviction is 5 years to 15 years. Appellant's scheduled conditional release date is August 29, 2017 and his maximum expiration date is August 29, 2022.

The guideline range established by the Division of Parole had a minimum of 22 months and a maximum of 40 months. Mr. _____ was credited with 55 months of total time served when he met with the Parole Board for his initial appearance on May 1, 2012. Appellant appeared before the Parole Board while he was at Gowanda Correctional Facility.

The Board denied parole and held Appellant for the maximum 24 months for the following reasons:

"DESPITE AN EARNED ELIGIBILITY CERTIFICATE, PAROLE IS DENIED. AFTER A PERSONAL INTERVIEW, RECORD

REVIEW AND DELIBERATION, IT IS THE DETERMINATION OF THIS PANEL THAT IF RELEASED AT THIS TIME, THERE IS A REASONABLE PROBABILITY THAT YOU WOULD NOT LIVE AT LIBERTY WITHOUT VIOLATING THE LAW. YOUR RELEASE AT THIS TIME IS INCOMPATIBLE WITH THE WELFARE AND SAFETY OF THE COMMUNITY. YOU APPEARED BEFORE THIS PANEL FOR THE SERIOUS INSTANT OFFENSES OF MANSLAUGHTER 2ND AND VEHICULAR ASSAULT 3RD. YOUR CRIMINAL RECORD RELFECTS NO PRIOR UNLAWFUL BEHAVIOR, HOWEVER, IT DOES NOT MINIMIZE THE SERIOUSNESS OF YOUR OFFENSES. YOUR ACTIONS CAUSED THE DEATH OF AN INNOCENT VICTIM. CONSIDERATION HAS BEEN GIVEN TO AN ASSESSMENT OF YOUR RISKS AND NEEDS FOR YOUR SUCCESS ON PAROLE. THE PANEL ALSO NOTES YOUR PROGRAMMING, GOOD DISCIPLINARY RECORD, RELEASE PLANS AND YOUR LETTERS OF SUPPORT. HOWEVER, DESPITE THESE ACCOMPLISHMENTS, WHEN CONSIDERING ALL RELEVANT FACTORS, DISCRETIONARY RELEASE IS NOT WARRANTED."

Appellant thereafter filed a timely notice of Appeal.

ARGUMENT

POINT I

THE PAROLE BOARD'S DECISION RESULTED IN STATUTORY VIOLATIONS, DENIAL OF APPELLANT'S CONSTITUTIONAL RIGHT TO DUE PROCESS, AND IS AFFECTED BY IRRATIONALITY BORDERING ON IMPROPRIETY.

It is not the role of the Parole Board to resentence Appellant according to the personal opinion of its members as to the appropriate penalty for manslaughter 2° and vehicular assault 3°. Here, the Judge did not intend for Appellant to serve more than the minimum term of 5 years which is indicated in the sentencing minutes. The Board's determination violated the statutory requirements set forth in Executive Law §§259—i and 259-c(4) which provide the standards that must be followed by the Board in determining whether to release the inmate to parole supervision.

Before making a parole release decision, the Executive Law requires the Board to consider certain factors. This criteria is mandatory, not discretionary, when utilized in assessing whether the applicant meets the criteria for parole release.

1.) Institutional Record

According to the first factor, under state law, the Board must consider a parole applicant's "institutional record including program goals and accomplishments, academic achievements, vocational education, training or work assignments, therapy and interpersonal relationships with staff and inmates," in assessing whether a prisoner meets the criteria for parole. Executive Law §259-i(2)(c)(a)(i). In the instant matter, the record reflects that Appellant has completed the Drug Alert and Aggression Replacement Training (ART) programs, obtained his G.E.D., and currently participates in the Alcoholics Anonymous (AA) and Driving While Intoxicated (DWI) programs. Clearly, the record reflects, and Appellant's institutional record shows that Appellant has successfully completed, or is enrolled in every program offered to him along with the work assignments. Hence, Appellant's fitness for parole. See Shephard v. Taylor, 556 F.2d 648, 652 (2d Cir.1977), quoting Moody v. Daggett, 429 U.S. 78, 88-90 (1976).

The Parole Board decision and determination denying Appellant's release was an abuse of discretion, and arbitrary and capricious as a matter of law in failing to accurately consider whether Appellant would pose a threat to society, or that he could not "remain at liberty without violating the law." See Watson v. Disabato, 393 F.Supp. 390-394 ("parole statutes provide that inmate shall be released unless information indicates substantial likelihood that such inmate would commit crimes if released. This creates a due process liberty interest"). Appellant's institutional record and accomplishments have been nothing but positive. This fact was acknowledged by the Parole Board in its denial of Appellant's parole release. Therefore, this factor weighs heavily in Appellant's favor.

2.) Temporary Release Program

Due to the nature of Appellant's instant offense, Appellant is ineligible to participate in the Temporary Release Program. Accordingly, this factor is neutral.

3.) Release Plans & Support

The third factor that state law requires for the Board to consider is "release plans including community resources, employment, education and training and support services available to the inmate." Executive Law §259-i(2)(c)(a)(iii). Appellant has the complete support of his family and friends, and intends to reside with his parents in Brooklyn, New York upon his release. In addition to this he has a reasonable letter of assurance of employment upon his release from his previous employer Universal Imaging Corp. as an ultrasound technician. Appellant also intends to participate in the DWI program being offered in his community upon his release. Appellant has also obtained several letters of support from Assemblyman Brad Usern (D), Brooklyn, New York, and several members of family and friends who are willing to support him upon his release. When taking all of this into consideration, this factor weighs heavily in Appellant's favor. The Board, however, did not acknowledge that this information was before them and further compounded their error by not basing its decision on a single one of these factors. In doing so, the Board failed to follow its own mandate which demands that these factors be considered. Silmon v. Travis, 95 N.Y.2d 470, 476-477 (2000).

4.) Deportation

Appellant is a naturalized citizen of the United States, therefore this factor is a neutral one.

5.) Victim Opposition/Statement

The Parole Board is also required to consider "any statement made to the Board by the crime victim or the victim's representative." Executive Law §259-i(2)(c)(A)(v). It is based upon information and belief that no such statement exists where Appellant is concerned. Therefore, in that regard, this factor is neutral. However, Appellant takes full accountability for his actions which resulted in the death of his victim without suggesting that his actions be excused or minimized.

6.) Seriousness of the Offense

State-law requires the Parole Board to consider a number of factors under the rubric "seriousness of the offense." These include the "seriousness of the offense with due consideration to the type of sentence, length of sentence and recommendations of the sentencing Court, the district attorney, the attorney for the inmate, the pre-sentence probation report, as well as consideration of any mitigating and aggravating factors, and activities following arrest, and prior to confinement. While the seriousness of the offense is a factor that the Board must consider, "when left with the seriousness of Appellant's offense as the exclusive factor considered and the sole basis for the Board's conclusion of nonrehabilitation and unreadiness for release, the conclusion is irrational, and contrary to the statutory discretion authorized." Coaxum v. New York State Bd. of Parole, 14 Misc.3d 661; Wallman v. Travis, 18 A.D.3d at 307-308.

7.) Prior Criminal Record

The Parole Board is mandated to consider an inmate's "prior criminal record, including the nature and pattern of the offenses, adjustment to any previous probation or parole supervision and institutional confinement." While the Parole Board may use the seriousness of the offense or the overall criminal record as the sole reason to deny parole, it must provide the parole applicant with aggravating factors which justify additional incarceration. The legislature "has not defined 'seriousness of [the] crime' in terms of specific categories of either crimes or victims and it is apparent that in order to preclude the granting of parole exclusively on this ground as was done here, there must have been some significantly aggravating or egregious circumstances surrounding the commission of the particular crime." Darryl King v. New York State Division of Parole, 190 A.D.2d 423 at 433 (1st Dept.1993), aff'd, Darryl King v. New York State Division of Parole, 83 N.Y.2d 788 (1994). In King, the court recognized that although he was convicted of murder, he was still entitled to a fair hearing as a matter of law.

In addition to this, "the mere reference to the violence of the crime, without elaboration, does not constitute the requisite aggravating circumstances beyond the inherent seriousness of the crime itself." Daniel Johnson v. New York State Division of Parole, 65 A.D.3d 838 (4th Dept.2009).

In the instant matter, the Parole Board erred because, in contrast to King, the Board failed to state any aggravating factors associated with Appellant's instant offense. The Board also did not "establish written procedures for its use in making Parole Board decisions as required by law," i.e., written procedures that incorporated the risks and needs principles to measure the rehabilitation of Appellant, the likelihood of Appellant's success upon release, and to assist the Board in determining whether Appellant may be released to parole supervision. Especially, where, as here, the Board noted Appellant's lack of a prior criminal record, its decision is clearly arbitrary and capricious. See Executive Law §259-c(4).

The record in this matter demonstrates unequivocally Appellant's insight into, and unambiguous remorse for the damage that was caused by his actions. Appellant has also expressed guilt and shame with regard to his crimes. Appellant completed the minimum sentence of 5 years in a manner far exceeding the mere performance of his duties or the things necessary to gain parole. Therefore, the Parole Board's decision to hold Appellant for an additional 24 months was excessive, and irrational bordering on impropriety.

A. There is a Strong Rehabilitative Component in the Executive Law that Requires Consideration.

On October 1, of 2011, the amendments to Executive Law became effective and required that the Board shall:

> "establish written procedures for its use in making parole decisions as required by law..Such written procedures shall incorporate risks and needs principles to measure the

rehabilitation of persons appearing before the board, the likelihood of success of such persons upon release, and assist members of the state board of parole in determining which inmates may be released to parole supervision."

(Emphasis Added).

Appellant appeared before the Parole Board after the effective date of the statutes' effectuation and the Division of Parole failed to establish written procedures that they were required by law to consider when making their determination whether to release Appellant to parole supervision or not. The Parole Board's brief reference to Appellant's "institutional accomplishments and release plans" are sufficient to satisfy the statutory mandate regarding parole release consideration. Executive Law §259-c(4); Wallman v. Travis, 18 A.D.3d 304, 308.

In addition to that, the Parole Board's decision to deny Appellant parole release is a conclusion that he is not rehabilitated. This conclusion is not supported by any factual finding or any established written procedures, thereby making it irrational and improper. Friedgood v. New York State Bd. Of Parole, 22 A.D.3d 950, 951.

When the Parole Board is presented with having to weigh the seriousness of the instant offense in determining whether a parole applicant still poses a danger to society, the New York State Court of Appeals has reasoned that there is a strong rehabilitative component inherent in the Executive Law that obligates the Parole Board to evaluate "petitioner's rehabilitative progress to see if he still posed a danger..." Silmon v. Travis, 95 N.Y.2d 470, 478 (2000); See Also Matter of Serrano v. Travis, Albany Co. Index No. 541-03, Slip Op., 9-22-03 ("the rehabilitative ideal is the cornerstone of indeterminate sentencing").

The legislative intent behind the addition of §259-c(4) to the Executive Law in 2011 is to require the Parole Board to evaluate an incarcerated individual's "rehabilitation" and their "likelihood of success... upon release" based on who they are today as opposed to the person they were years ago when they committed their crime. Appellant's case was handled by the Parole Board without those considerations being balanced during their decision-making process. Guerin v. New York State Div. of Parole, 276 A.D.2d 899, 900.

In Matter of Thwaites v. NYS Bd. of Parole, NY Slip Op., 21453 (Orange Co.2011), Justice Ecker stated that the Parole Board, in denying Thwaites release to parole supervision, relied on "past focused rhetoric, not future-focused risk assessment analysis." Justice Ecker ruled that:

- "The Court finds the Board's decision denying parole in this case to be arbitrary and capricious, irrational, and improper based upon the parole board's failure to articulate any rational, non conclusory basis, other than its reliance on the seriousness of the crime."

Mr. Thwaites was serving a 25 year to life sentence for murder and assault, and although he appeared before the Board prior to the effective date of Executive Law §259-c(4), the Court directed that the Parole Board afford Mr. Thwaites a new parole hearing wherein the rehabilitation factor is applied retroactively. This rationale was again utilized in the Matter of Valesquez v. NYS Board of Parole, Index No. 6271-11 (Orange Co.2012).

Here, the board's determination fails to conform with state law as its decision is conclusory and fails to reveal reasoning. It also fails to explain how and why Appellant's instant offense, combined with all the other factors that are required precludes Appellant's release. This failure is further compounded by lack of established written procedures in place for the Parole Board to follow at his hearing and during the appeal process as required by law.

Clearly, the Board's conclusion must be supported with consideration of the statutory factors under Executive Law §§ 259—i(2)(C)(A), and 259-c(4) other than the seriousness of his crime, "the factors bearing on parole, not on the penalty for the offense determined by the legislature and the court." King v. New York State Div. of Parole, 83 N.Y.2d 788, 790-791.

CONCLUSION

For the above stated reasons, Appellant should be paroled forthwith, or in the alternative, be provided with a de novo hearing in front of a different panel, in which the Board must fairly consider each of the mandatory factors.

Respectfully submitted,

_____

_____ # _____
Petitioner Pro Se
Gowanda Correctional Facility
P.O. Box 311
Gowanda NY 14070

Sworn to before me this
_____ day of _____ 20___.

_____

ARTICLE 78 PROCEEDINGS

Article 78 of the Civil Practice Law and Rules (CPLR) governs proceedings that are used to challenge administrative decisions of state and local government agencies based upon their actions or their failure to perform certain actions. In this Volume we are dealing solely with the challenge of an administrative decision of the New York State Division of Parole as an example.

There are generally two types of Article 78 proceedings, i.e., "mandamus" and "prohibition." The "mandamus to compel" is a vehicle used to have the court order an officer or body to "perform a specified ministerial act that is required by law to be performed." Hamptons Hosp. & Med. Center, Inc. v. Moore, 52 N.Y.2d 88, 96, 436 N.Y.S.2d 239, 243 (1981). "Prohibition" is a vehicle utilized to "restrain judicial or quasi-judicial officers from acting without jurisdiction or in excess of their jurisdiction." Town of Huntington v. New York State Div. of Human Rights, 82 N.Y.2d 783, 604 N.Y.S.2d 541 (1993).

EXHAUSTING YOUR REMEDIES

Before you can utilize an Article 78 proceeding to challenge an administrative decision, all administrative remedies must be exhausted. This means that every issue must have been appealed through the proper channels until every officer designated to administratively hear the claim(s) has done so. Once that occurs the agency decision becomes final. Start working on your argument for your Article 78 before the decision becomes final. This way, if the decision is not in your favor and the 120 days you will have to file the Article 78 in is not enough time for you, you will have a head start in preparing your paperwork. Even the highly skilled pro se litigant knows that they must do the proper research in advance to make it easier for them when it comes time to file motions.

QUESTIONS RAISED

Under the rules of CPLR §7803 there are four legal questions that may be raised in an Article 78 proceeding.

(a) Did the official render an unlawful decision?

Whenever an administrative decision is made in violation of a clearly established lawful procedure, you can challenge it in an Article 78 proceeding once you have exhausted your remedies. For this purpose, Article 78 has what is known as the "arbitrary and capricious" or "abuse of discretion" standards. The Court of Appeals has held that "arbitrary action is without sound basis in reason and is generally taken without regard to the facts." Pell v. Board of Education, 34 N.Y.2d 222, 356 N.Y.S.2d 833 (1974).

The sample arguments we have provided here pertaining to a mock parole board hearing utilize the "irrationality bordering on impropriety" standard being used as a basis to challenge the board's administrative decision to hold someone in prison for an additional 24 months without following their own procedures.

(b) Did the official fail to perform its lawful duty?

In determining whether an agency violated lawful procedure, the reviewing court will have to look at the rules, regulations and statutes that are supposed to be followed by a particular body or agency. It will be up to you as the litigant to find out what these regulations are and argue them from the beginning stages in order to properly exhaust them and give the court jurisdiction to entertain your Article 78 petition. If an agency fails to follow their own rules and regulations in making a decision you will have to clearly point that out in order to get the court to vacate or annul their decision.

(c) Was the official's decision based on substantial evidence?

The "substantial evidence" standard of an Article 78 proceeding makes it mandatory that the 78 petition be transferred to the Appellate Division for review because a case involving an issue of substantial evidence cannot be decided by a justice of the Supreme Court under CPLR §7804. Once the Supreme Court judge reviews your petition and recognizes that it includes a substantial evidence issue they will automatically transfer the proceedings to the Appellate Division for the department that has jurisdiction over that particular court. When the Appellate Division reviews the case it must determine whether the agency's findings are "supported by the kind of evidence on which responsible persons are accustomed to rely on in serious affairs." People ex rel. Vega v. Smith, 66 N.Y.2d 130, 495 N.Y.S.2d 332 (1985).

(d) Did the officials proceed in excess of its jurisdiction?

One of the issues currently being raised is whether the Parole Board is proceeding in excess of its jurisdiction in cases where the new amendments that became effective on October 1, 2011 have yet to be implemented. It will take a while for the appellate courts to settle the issue(s) that are surfacing because the lower courts are split. Especially when it comes to the issue of whether the new amendments to the judiciary law should be applied retroactively.

WHERE TO FILE AN ARTICLE 78

An Article 78 proceeding can be filed in the county where the events complained of occurred; (2) the state official made the decision complained of; and (3) where the Chief Officer of the agency you are complaining of has its principal office. CPLR § 506(b).

The New York State Division of Parole [Community Supervision] has its principal office in Albany, New York. Therefore, a prisoner who is challenging a parole board hearing that was held at Clinton in Dannemora, New York can either file their petition in Clinton county where their hearing was held, or they can file in Albany county where the principal office is.

WHAT TO FILE

(1) Cover letter to the court clerk explaining exactly what papers you are forwarding along with the letter to be filed with the court.

(2) Application for an index number which is a form that should be available in the law library. One can also be obtained from the clerk of the court that you intend to file your petition in.

(3) Request for Judicial Intervention (RJI) form which must be a part of your package to enable the court clerk to assign

your case to a Supreme Court Judge. These forms should also be available at facility law libraries. If not you can write to the county clerk where you intend to file your petition and request them.

(4) Affidavit in Support of Order to Show Cause is an affidavit attesting to why the respondent should "show cause" as to why the petitioner shouldn't obtain the relief they are seeking. A notice of petition must be personally served upon each respondent. In the case of a petitioner who is incarcerated, they must opt for the order to show cause due to their inability to serve the papers themselves. We have included a Sample Petition to show the format.

(5) Petition, which is the body of the motion outlining your arguments and the reasons why you think you should prevail on your claim(s). It is here that you make reference to the cases, rules and regulations, and statutes you are relying on as well as your exhibits. * If you make reference to exhibits or affidavits always remember to attach them to your motion so the judge handling your case can review them.

(6) Verification, is a sworn statement attesting that the information in your petition is true. If you are not absolutely certain about something in the petition you should state that it is "based upon information and belief" rather than swearing to something you are not 100% sure of.

(7) Poor person application, is an application to the court to proceed as a poor person in your Article 78 proceeding due to your inability to pay the filing fees. If the court grants your application you will have to pay anywhere from $15 to $50 if you are incarcerated, depending on how much money was in the institutional account in the past 6 months. All others must pay the full filing fee. If you are granted the reduced filing fee, the institution will process the money from your account and forward it to the court.

(8) Authorization Form - gives the institution the authorization to send the court clerk an individual's institutional account information of the past 5 months. It is also an acknowledgement that you have to pay the court fees and that you also give the institutional authorities the authorization to deduct the filing fees from the institutional account.

WHAT TO EXPECT AFTER YOU FILE

After you send all of the appropriate papers to the Court your case will be assigned to a judge who will decide whether or not to grant your poor person application. The judge will also issue a signed Order to Show Cause which will direct who you must serve with a copy of your motion and the Court's Order To Show Cause. It will also give you a deadline which your papers have to be served and give the respondent a deadline in which it has to respond. It will also include the date by which you have to send the original "proof of service" back to the Court indicating that you have served all the parties and the Attorney General's office in a timely manner.

You should notarize and copy an Affidavit of Service at the same time you make copies of the Court's Order to Show Cause so you can mail it to the Court at the same time you are mailing the papers to the respondents and the Attorney General at: Attorney General of the State of New York, Department of Law, The Capitol, Albany, New York, 12224.

Once you serve your papers you will eventually receive an Answer to your motion from the attorney general's office. You don't have to respond to it, however, you can and should always respond with what is called a "Reply Affidavit." A reply affidavit has to be submitted within five (5) days after you receive the Answer. Once all the papers are filed it usually takes 6 to 8 weeks for a judge to render a decision. However, it can take less time or longer depending on the judge's caseload and how long it will take for them to write the decision. If the judge happens to give you an unfavorable decision you can appeal it to the appellate division.

SUPREME COURT OF THE STATE OF NEW YORK
SUPREME COURT : ALBANY COUNTY
--X
In the Matter of the Application of

_____, #_____

                                (SAMPLE)
                              AFFIDAVIT IN SUPPORT
       Petitioner,   **OF ORDER TO SHOW**
                                CAUSE

For a Judgment Pursuant to Article 78
of the Civil Practice Law and Rules.

        -against-

THE NEW YORK STATE DIVISION OF PAROLE

              Respondent.
--X
STATE OF NEW YORK   )
)ss. :
COUNTY OF ERIE   )

     I, _____,
being duly sworn depose and say:
    1. I am the Petitioner in the above entitled proceeding.
    2. I make this affidavit in support of my Petition pursuant to Article 78 of the Civil Practice Law and Rules that this Court annul the determination made by the New York State Board of Parole that: denied parole and

held Petitioner for the maximum 24 months and failed to determine whether Petitioner presented a current danger based on all of the relevant statutory factors in violation of the Petitioner's fundamental right to due process of law under the constitution of this State and the Constitution of the United States. Executive Law §§259-i(1)(a), (2)(C)(A), and 259-c(4); N.Y. Constit., Art. I, §6; U.S. Constit., 14th Amend.

3. On May 1st, 2012 Petitioner appeared before the Parole Board and the Board denied parole and held Petitioner for the maximum 24 months.

4. At the time such hearing was held, the Board violated lawful procedure by making its decision without fairly considering each of the applicable factors mandated for consideration.

5. Petitioner seeks to proceed by Order to Show Cause rather than by Notice of Petition because the Board has the unquestionable duty to fairly consider each of the statutory requirements enumerated in Executive Law §259-i and incorporate the risks and needs principles to measure Petitioner's rehabilitation and his likelihood of success upon release in accordance with the dictates of Executive Law §259-c(4).

6. Petitioner being incarcerated, also cannot effect personal service of the within papers and respectfully requests that timely service of the within papers by mail be deemed sufficient.

7. Petitioner designates Albany county as the place of venue.

8. No previous application for the relief requested herein has been made.

9. I have moved by the annexed affidavit for a reduction/waiver of the filing fees.

WHEREFORE, Petitioner respectfully prays that this Court enter an Order directing Respondent to show cause why a judgment should not be made and entered pursuant to Article 78 of the Civil Practice Law and Rules annulling Respondent's determination to hold a hearing that failed to consider each of the mandatory factors and relied exclusively on the seriousness of the instant offense to deny parole; and Directing Respondent to hold a de novo hearing in front of a different panel in which the Board must show some aggravating circumstances, or explain why Respondent departed from the applicable standard, together with such other and further relief which this Court deems just and proper.

Respectfully submitted,

_____ # _____
Petitioner Pro Se
Gowanda Correctional Facility
P.O. Box 311
Gowanda NY 14070

Sworn to before me this
_____ day of _____ 20___.

SUPREME COURT OF THE STATE OF NEW YORK
SUPREME COURT : ALBANY COUNTY
--X
In the Matter of the Application of
_____, #_____

(SAMPLE)

VERIFIED PETITION

Petitioner,

For a Judgment Pursuant to Article 78
of the Civil Practice Law and Rules.

-against-

THE NEW YORK STATE DIVISION OF PAROLE

Respondent.
--X

TO:THE SUPREME COURT OF THE STATE OF NEW YORK

THE PETITION of _____ seeks a writ of mandamus under Article 78 of the Civil Practice Law and Rules challenging administrative actions taken against the Petitioner by the New York State Division of Parole which failed to consider each of the mandatory factors and relied exclusively on the seriousness of the instant offense to deny parole; and for an Order and Judgment reversing Respondent's May 1st, 2011 determination denying parole release and compelling Respondent, the New York State

Division of Parole to release Petitioner to parole supervision, or, in the alternative, to direct Respondent to hold a de novo hearing and render a decision consistent with the tenor of the Court's order.

PRELIMINARY STATEMENT

1. Petitioner was convicted after a jury trial of manslaughter 2° and vehicular assault. The basis for Petitioner's challenge of the denial of parole release is that Respondent's determination is clearly arbitrary, capricious, and failed to satisfy the statutory requirements for parole release consideration. As will be demonstrated, in light of the Board's violation of lawful procedure by failing to consider each of the mandatory factors, the Board's exclusive reliance on the instant offense to deny parole is clearly "irrationality bordering on impropriety."

2. Petitioner filed a timely notice of appeal and briefs outlining his arguments upon the New York State Division of Parole Appeal's Unit in Albany, New York resulting in a blanket denial. Therefore, venue for this special proceeding lies in this Court.

3. The guideline range established by the Division of Parole for Petitioner is a minimum of 22 months and a maximum of 40 months. Petitioner has served well over his guideline range.

ARGUMENT

POINT I

THE PAROLE BOARD'S DECISION RESULTED IN STATUTORY VIOLATIONS, DENIAL OF PETITIONER'S CONSTITUTIONAL RIGHT TO DUE PROCESS, AND IS AFFECTED BY IRRATIONALITY BORDERING ON IMPROPRIETY.

4. It is not the role of the parole Board to resentence Petitioner according to the personal opinion of its members as to the appropriate penalty for manslaughter 2° and vehicular assault 3°. Here, the Judge did not intend for Petitioner to serve more than the minimum term of 5 years which is indicated in the sentencing minutes. The Board's determination violated the statutory requirements set forth in Executive Law §§259—i and 259-c(4) which provide the standards that must be followed by the Board in determining whether to release the inmate to parole supervision.

5. Before making a parole release decision, the Executive Law requires the Board to consider certain factors. This criteria is mandatory, not discretionary, when utilized in assessing whether the applicant meets the criteria for parole release.

1.) Institutional Record

6. According to the first factor, under state law, the Board must consider a parole applicant's "institutional record including program goals and accomplishments, academic achievements, vocational education, training or work assignments, therapy and interpersonal relationships with staff and inmates," in assessing whether a prisoner meets the criteria for parole. Executive Law §259-i(2)(c)(a)(i). In the instant matter, the record reflects that Petitioner has completed the Drug Alert and Aggression Replacement Training (ART) programs, obtained his G.E.D., and currently participates in the Alcoholics Anonymous (AA) and Driving While Intoxicated (DWI) programs. Clearly, the record reflects, and Petitioner's institutional record shows that Petitioner has successfully completed, or is enrolled in every program offered to him along with the work assignments. Hence, Petitioner's fitness for parole. See Shephard v. Taylor, 556 F.2d 643, 652 (2d Cir.1977), quoting Moody v. Daggett, 429 U.S. 78, 88-90 (1976).

7. The Parole Board decision and determination denying Petitioner's release was an abuse of discretion, and arbitrary and capricious as a matter of law in failing to accurately consider whether Petitioner would pose a threat to society, or that he could not "remain at liberty without violating the law." See Watson v. Disabato, 393 F.Supp. 390-394 ("parole statutes provide that

inmate shall be released unless information indicates substantial likelihood that such inmate would commit crimes if released. This creates a due process liberty interest").

8. Petitioner's institutional record and accomplishments have been nothing but positive. This fact was acknowledged by the Parole Board in its denial of Petitioner's parole release. Therefore, this factor weighs heavily in Petitioner's favor.

2.) Temporary Release Program

9. Due to the nature of Petitioner's instant offense, Petitioner is ineligible to participate in the Temporary Release Program. Accordingly, this factor is neutral.

3.) Release Plans & Support

10. The third factor that state law requires for the Board to consider is "release plans including community resources, employment, education and training and support services available to the inmate." Executive Law § 259-i(2)(c)(a)(iii). Petitioner has the complete support of his family and friends, and intends to reside with his parents in Brooklyn, New York upon his release. In addition to this he has a reasonable letter of assurance of employment upon his release from his previous employer Universal Imaging Corp. as an ultrasound technician. Petitioner also intends to participate in the DWI program being offered in his community upon his release. Petitioner has also obtained

several letters of support from Assemblyman Brad Usern (D), Brooklyn, New York, and several members of family and friends who are willing to support him upon his release.

11. When taking all of this into consideration, this factor weighs heavily in Petitioner's favor. The Board, however, did not acknowledge that this information was before them and further compounded their error by not basing its decision on a single one of these factors. In doing so, the Board failed to follow its own mandate which demands that these factors be considered. Silmon v. Travis, 95 N.Y.2d 470, 476-477 (2000).

4.) Deportation

12. Petitioner is a naturalized citizen of the United States, therefore this factor is a neutral one.

5.) Victim Opposition/Statement

13. The Parole Board is also required to consider "any statement made to the Board by the crime victim or the victim's representative." Executive Law §259—i(2)(c)(A)(v). It is based upon information and belief that no such statement exists where Petitioner is concerned. Therefore, in that regard, this factor is neutral. However, Petitioner takes full accountability for his actions which resulted in the death of his victim without suggesting that his actions be excused or minimized.

6.) Seriousness of the Offense

14. State-law requires the Parole Board to consider a number of factors under the rubric "seriousness of the offense." These include the "seriousness of the offense with due consideration to the type of sentence, length of sentence and recommendations of the sentencing Court, the district attorney, the attorney for the inmate, the pre-sentence probation report, as well as consideration of any mitigating and aggravating factors, and activities following arrest, and prior to confinement. While the seriousness of the offense is a factor that the Board must consider, "when left with the seriousness of Petitioner's offense as the exclusive factor considered and the sole basis for the Board's conclusion of nonrehabilitation and unreadiness for release, the conclusion is irrational, and contrary to the statutory discretion authorized." Coaxum v. New York State Bd. of Parole, 14 Misc.3d 661; Wallman v. Travis, 18 A.D.3d at 307-308.

7.) Prior Criminal Record

15. The Parole Board is mandated to consider an inmates "prior criminal record, including the nature and pattern of the offenses, adjustment to any previous probation or parole supervision and institutional confinement." While the Parole Board may use the seriousness of the offense or the overall criminal record as the sole reason to deny parole, it must provide the

parole applicant with aggravating factors which justify additional incarceration. The legislature "has not defined 'seriousness of [the] crime' in terms of specific categories of either crimes or victims and it is apparent that in order to preclude the granting of parole exclusively on this ground as was done here, there must have been some significantly aggravating or egregious circumstances surrounding the commission of the particular crime." Darryl King v. New York State Division of Parole, 190 A.D.2d 423 at 433 (1st Dept.1993), aff'd, Darryl King v. New York State Division of Parole, 83 N.Y.2d 788 (1994). In King, the court recognized that although he was convicted of murder, he was still entitled to a fair hearing as a matter of law.

16. In addition to this, "the mere reference to the violence of the crime, without elaboration, does not constitute the requisite aggravating circumstances beyond the inherent seriousness of the crime itself." Daniel Johnson v. New York State Division of Parole, 65 A.D.3d 838 (4th Dept.2009).

17. In the instant matter, the Parole Board erred because, in contrast to King, the Board failed to state any aggravating factors associated with Petitioner's instant offense. The Board also did not "establish written procedures for its use in making Parole Board decisions as required by law," i.e., written procedures that incorporated

the risks and needs principles to measure the rehabilitation of Petitioner, the likelihood of Petitioner's success upon release, and to assist the Board in determining whether Petitioner may be released to parole supervision. Especially, where, as here, the Board noted Petitioner's lack of a prior criminal record, its decision is clearly arbitrary and capricious. See Executive Law §259-c(4).

18. The record in this matter demonstrates unequivocally, Petitioner's insight into, and unambiguous remorse for the damage that was caused by his actions. Petitioner has also expressed guilt and shame with regard to his crimes. Petitioner completed the minimum sentence of 5 years in a manner far exceeding the mere performance of his duties or the things necessary to gain parole. Therefore, the Parole Board's decision to hold Petitioner for an additional 24 months was excessive, and irrational bordering on impropriety.

A. There is a Strong Rehabilitative Component in the Executive Law that Requires Consideration.

19. On October 1, of 2011, the amendments to Executive Law became effective and required that the Board shall:

> "establish written procedures for its use in making parole decisions as required by law..Such written procedures shall incorporate risks

and needs principles to measure the rehabilitation of persons appearing before the board, the likelihood of success of such persons upon release, and assist members of the state board of parole in determining which inmates may be released to parole supervision."

(Emphasis Added).

20. Petitioner appeared before the Parole Board after the effective date of the statutes' effectuation and the Division of Parole failed to establish written procedures that they were required by law to consider when making their determination whether to release Petitioner to parole supervision or not. The Parole Board's brief reference to Petitioner's "institutional accomplishments and release plans" are sufficient to satisfy the statutory mandate regarding parole release consideration. Executive Law §259-c(4); Wallman v. Travis, 18 A.D.3d 304, 308.

21. In addition to that, the Parole Board's decision to deny Petitioner parole release is a conclusion that he is not rehabilitated. This conclusion is not supported by any factual finding or any established written procedures, thereby making it irrational and improper. Friedgood v. New York State Bd. Of Parole, 22 A.D.3d 950, 951.

22. When the Parole Board is presented with having to weigh the seriousness of the instant offense in determining whether

a parole applicant still poses a danger to society, the New York State Court of Appeals has reasoned that there is a strong rehabilitative component inherent in the Executive Law that obligates the Parole Board to evaluate "petitioner's rehabilitative progress to see if he still posed a danger..." Silmon v. Travis, 95 N.Y.2d 470, 478 (2000); See Also Matter of Serrano v. Travis, Albany Co. Index No. 541-03, Slip Op., 9-22-03 ("the rehabilitative ideal is the cornerstone of indeterminate sentencing").

23. The legislative intent behind the addition of §259-c(4) to the Executive Law in 2011 is to require the Parole Board to evaluate an incarcerated individual's "rehabilitation" and their "likelihood of success...upon release" based on who they are today as opposed to the person they were years ago when they committed their crime. Petitioner's case was handled by the Parole Board without those considerations being balanced during their decision-making process. Guerin v. New York State Div. of Parole, 276 A.D.2d 899, 900.

24. In Matter of Thwaites v. NYS Bd. of Parole, NY Slip Op., 21453 (Orange Co.2011), Justice Ecker stated that the Parole Board, in denying Thwaites release to parole supervision, relied on "past focused rhetoric, not future-focused risk assessment analysis." Justice Ecker ruled that:

"The Court finds the Board's decision denying parole in this case to be arbitrary and capricious, irrational, and improper based upon the parole board's failure to articulate any rational, non conclusory basis, other than its reliance on the seriousness of the crime."

25. Mr. Thwaites was serving a 25 year to life sentence for murder and assault, and although he appeared before the Board prior to the effective date of Executive Law §259-c(4), the Court directed that the Parole Board afford Mr. Thwaites a new parole hearing wherein the rehabilitation factor is applied retroactively. This rationale was again utilized in the Matter of Valesquez v. NYS Board of Parole, Index No. 6271-11 (Orange Co.2012).

26. Here, the board's determination fails to conform with state law as its decision is conclusory and fails to reveal reasoning. It also fails to explain how and why Petitioner's instant offense, combined with all the other factors that are required precludes Petitioner's release. This failure is further compounded by lack of established written procedures in place for the Parole Board to follow at his hearing and during the appeal process as required by law.

27. Clearly, the Board's conclusion must be supported with consideration of the statutory factors under Executive Law

§§259-i(2)(C)(A), and 259-c(4) other than the seriousness of his crime, "the factors bearing on parole, not on the penalty for the offense determined by the legislature and the court." King v. New York State Div. of Parole, 83 N.Y.2d 788, 790-791.

CONCLUSION

WHEREFORE, Petitioner respectfully prays that this Court enter an Order; Directing Respondent to show cause why a judgment should not be made and entered pursuant to Article 78 of the Civil Practice Law and Rules annulling Respondent's determination to hold a parole hearing that failed to review each of the applicable factors mandated for consideration; and Directing Respondent to hold a de novo hearing in front of a different panel in which the Board must fairly consider each of the applicable factors mandated, including the rehabilitation factor, together with such other and further relief which the Court deems just and proper.

Dated: _____ _____, 20____.

                    Respectfully submitted,

                    _____

                    _____ # _____

                    Petitioner Pro Se
                    Gowanda Correctional Facility
                    P.O. Box 311
                    Gowanda NY 14070

VERIFICATION

STATE OF NEW YORK)
)ss.:
COUNTY OF ERIE)

_____, being duly sworn, deposes and says that I am the Petitioner in the herewithin action, that I have read the foregoing Petition and know the contents thereof, that the same is true to my knowledge, except as to those matters stated upon information and belief, and those matters I believe to be true.

Respectfully submitted,

_____

_____ #_____
Petitioner Pro Se
Gowanda Correctional Facility
P.O. Box 311
Gowanda NY 14070

Sworn to before me this
_____ day of _____ 20___.

_____

APPEALING AN ARTICLE 78 DECISION

If your Article 78 petition was dismissed, transferred to the Appellate Division because it raised a "substantial evidence" issue, or your relief was denied in whole or in part by the reviewing Court, your next step is to file an appeal of the decision. In the case of a substantial evidence issue, your next step will be to file your brief with the Court, the County Attorney of the County of the county you are filing your appeal in, and the attorney for respondent which is either the Attorney General of the State of New York, or Corporation Counsel in New York City. In cases where your Article 78 was denied or dismissed and you have to appeal the decision, you have 30 days from the date you receive the decision to appeal. Your motion will consist:

(1) Notice of Appeal; and
(2) Notice Of Motion To Proceed As A Poor Person, And For Assignment of Counsel; and
(3) Affidavit In Support of Motion For Poor Person Relief.

We have provided a Blank Motion as a guide to show our readers the format of the motion for appealing an Article 78 decision. We have also included a Sample Brief dealing with parole issues showing the format and structure of a brief. If your petition was transferred to the Appellate Division or your appeal application is granted, you will have to file a brief. The rules vary depending on where you have to file so you should check the New York Rules of Court for the rules of that particular Division you are in. Also you can attach the decision you are appealing from as an exhibit. *It should be noted that if you are filing a brief in the Fourth Department, they are very strict about their rule requiring the cover of the brief to include "On Submission By <u>Your Name</u>" in the upper right hand corner.

When you file your appeal with the Court be sure to send an original "Affidavit of Service" showing that the County Attorney and the Attorney General were served with a copy of your motion papers. Once your appeal is granted, the Court will notify you of how many copies of your brief you must file along with your original to the Court, and how many copies you must serve upon the attorney for the respondent. They will also set the time limit on when your briefs must be filed and served and when the attorney for respondent must answer your papers by. You can file a Reply Brief in accordance with the Court's rules within five days if there is something in the answer that you disagree with. After all papers are received regarding the matter the Court will hear your arguments on submission and then render a decision.

You should submit your appeal application within 25 days of receiving the Court's decision. You should also begin drafting your brief up in anticipation of an unfavorable decision of your Article 78 Petition to make it that much easier for you to prepare one if you have to eventually. If you receive an unfavorable decision on appeal you can file for leave to appeal to the Court of Appeals which is the next step in the appellate process. We have included a Sample Leave To Appeal Application in our chapter on the Court of Appeals. *Always remember that you should be vigilant in pursuit of championing your legal cause on your own behalf or on behalf of others. It takes a lot of patience when dealing with the law from "the other side." And you don't have to be in prison to be on the other side. Even if you are in society and you are not living right you are on the other side, and are one crime away from being on the other side, or the inside of a prison cell. Gorilla Lawfair isn't designed to show individuals ways that may help them get out of prison. It is written with the hope that individuals will also build character in seeing how difficult it is to get out of trouble and do themselves some justice by "staying out" of prison.

SUPREME COURT OF THE STATE OF NEW YORK
APPELLATE DIVISION: _____ DEPARTMENT
------------------------------------X
In the Matter of the Application of

_____, #_____

Petitioner-Appellant,   **NOTICE OF APPEAL**

For a Judgment Pursuant   Index #_____
to Article 78 of the Civil
Practice Law and Rules.   RJI #_____

     -against-

THE NEW YORK STATE DIVISION OF PAROLE

     Respondents.
------------------------------------X

PERSONS:

    PLEASE TAKE NOTICE, that the above named petitioner, _____, hereby appeals to the Appellate Division in and for the _____ Department, from a Judgment entered by the Hon. _____, J., _____ County Supreme Court, in the above entitled action in the office of the Clerk of _____ County on _____ _____ 20___, dismissing the petition brought pursuant to Article 78 of the Civil Practice Law and Rules. This appeal is taken from each and every part of the aforementioned judgment as well as the whole thereof.

Dated: _____, ____, 20__ .
       _____, New York

                    Yours etc.,

                    _____
                    _____ # _____
                    Petitioner Pro Se

                    _____
                    _____
                    _____

SUPREME COURT OF THE STATE OF NEW YORK
APPELLATE DIVISION: _____ DEPARTMENT
--X
In the Matter of the Application of

_____, # _____

Petitioner-Appellant, **NOTICE OF MOTION
TO PROCEED AS A**
For a Judgment Pursuant **POOR PERSON, AND**
to Article 78 of the Civil **FOR ASSIGNMENT OF**
Practice Law and Rules. **COUNSEL**

-against-

THE NEW YORK STATE DIVISION OF PAROLE

Respondents.
--X
SIRS:

PLEASE TAKE NOTICE, that upon the annexed affidavit of _____, duly sworn to on the _____ day of _____, 20___, and all proceedings held previously, a motion will be made in the Supreme Court of the State of New York, Appellate Division, _____ Judicial Department thereof, at the Courthouse located at _____, on the _____ day of _____, 20___, at 9:30 a.m. for an Order:

1. Permitting the petitioner to prosecute an appeal on the original record as a

poor person from the determination of the respondent on the ground(s) that petitioner has insufficient income and property and is unable to pay the costs, fees and expenses necessary to prosecute said appeal;

2. Assigning counsel to prosecute said appeal; and

3. For such other and further relief as to this Court may seem just and proper.

Dated: _____ _____, 20___

        Yours etc.,

        _____

        _____ #_____
        Appellant Pro Se

        _____

        _____

        _____

TO: Clerk of the Court for
    Appellate Division, _____ Department

    County Attorney of _____ County

    Attorney General
    Of the State of New York
    Department of Law
    The Capitol
    Albany, NY 12224

SUPREME COURT OF THE STATE OF NEW YORK
APPELLATE DIVISION: _____ DEPARTMENT
--X
In the Matter of the Application of

_____, # _____

    Petitioner-Appellant,　　**AFFIDAVIT IN**
　　　　　　　　　　　　　　　　　　SUPPORT OF MOTION
For a Judgment Pursuant　　**FOR POOR PERSON**
to Article 78 of the　　　　**RELIEF**
Civil Practice Law and
Rules.

    -against-

THE NEW YORK STATE DIVISION OF PAROLE

        Respondents.
--X
STATE OF NEW YORK　　)
　　　　　　　　　　　　)ss. :
COUNTY OF ERIE　　　　)

_____, being duly sworn, deposes and says that:
    1. I am a prisoner incarcerated in the state of New York at _____.
    2. I am about to commence an appeal to the Appellate Division of the New York state Supreme Court in the _____ Department from a judgment entered by the Hon. _____,
Supreme Court, _____,

County, in the above entitled action in the office of the Clerk of _____ County on _____ _____, 20___, dismissing the petition brought by petitioner pursuant to Article 78 of the Civil Practice Law and Rules. The appeal is taken from each and every part of said judgment as well as the whole thereof.

 3. I make this application pursuant to §1101 of the Civil Practice Law and Rules upon the grounds that I am unable to pay the costs, fees and expenses necessary to prosecute this action.

 4. I have no real property, no substantial personal property, no bank accounts, and no other person is beneficially interested in any recovery sought in this proceeding.

 5. My weekly pay is $_____._____.

 6. I have $_____._____ in my inmate account.

 7. I will be unable to prosecute this action or prepare all the documents required unless I am permitted to do so as a poor person.

 8. I do not know of any attorney who is willing to represent me in this proceeding, and therefore desire that an attorney of suitable experience be assigned to represent me in this proceeding without compensation.

 9. That no previous application for the relief sought herein has been made.

WHEREFORE, I pray that I be permitted:

(a) to prosecute this action as a poor person;
(b) to appeal on the original record; and
(c) that the Court assign a suitable attorney to represent me for that purpose.

_____
_____ # _____
Appellant Pro Se
_____ Correctional Facility

_____
_____ NY _____

Sworn to before me this
_____ day of _____ 20____.
_____

AFFIDAVIT OF SERVICE

STATE OF NEW YORK)
)ss.:
COUNTY OF _____)

_____, being duly sworn, deposes and says:
   That he/she has prepared the enclosed Notice of Appeal, Notice of Motion to Proceed as a Poor Person, and for Assignment of Counsel, and Affidavit in Support of Motion for Poor Person Relief, and Notice of Entry, and has caused such to be forwarded through the mailroom at _____ Correctional Facility via U.S. Postal Service, first class mail to the following on _____ _____, 20___ :

1. Attorney General   2. _____
   Of the State of New   County Attorney
   YorkDepartment of Law   _____
   The Capitol   _____
   Albany, NY 12224   _____

                    _____
                    _____ # _____
                    Appellant Pro Se
                    _____ Correctional Facility
                    _____
                    _____ NY _____

Sworn to before me this
_____ day of _____ 20___.
_____

ANPU UNNEFER AMEN

AD No. _____

                                    To Be Submitted

STATE OF NEW YORK   SUPREME COURT
APPELLATE DIVISION   _____ DEPARTMENT

In the Matter of _____, # _____

            Appellant

         -against-

THE NEW YORK STATE DIVISION OF PAROLE,

            Respondent.

For a Judgment Pursuant to Article 78
of the Civil Practice Law and Rules.

Index No. _____

****
                  (SAMPLE)
              APPELLANT'S BRIEF
****

            _____
            _____ # _____
            Appellant Pro Se
            _____ Correctional Facility
            _____
            _____ NY _____

CONTENTS

Table Of Authorities 263
Preliminary Statement 265
Questions Presented 266
Statement Of The Case 266
Argument 275
Point I 275
     The Parole Board's Usage Of Appellant's Youthful Offender Adjudication To Deny Parole Release Deprived Appellant Of His Constitutional Right To Due Process Of Law And Is Affected By Irrationality Bordering On Impropriety. 275
Point II 277
     The Parole Board's Consideration Of Inaccurate Information Resulted In A Denial Of Petitioner's Constitutional Right To Due Process And Is Affected By Irrationality Bordering On Impropriety. 277
Point III 280
     The Parole Board In Its Decision Failed Qualitatively To Determine Whether Appellant Presented A Current Danger To Society Based

  On All Of The Relevant Statutory Factors
In Abdication Of Its Statutory Duty. 280
Point IV 284
  The Remedial Amendments To Executive Law
§259-I[2][C] And Executive Law §259-C[4]
Should Be Applied To This Proceeding
Retroactively. 284
Conclusion...286

TABLE OF AUTHORITIES

CASES

Burr v. Goord, 283 A.D.2d 891 (3rd Dept.2001) 279
Friedgood v. NYS Board of Parole, 22 A.D.3d 950, 951 281
Gleason v. Vee, 96 N.Y.2d 117, 122 (2001) 285
Hughes v. NYS Div. of Parole, 21 A.D.3d 1176,
1177 (3rd Dept.2005) 275
Lewis v. Travis, 9 A.D.3d 800 (3rd Dept.2004) 279
Majewski v. Broadalbin-Perth Cent. School District,
91 N.Y.2d 577 (1998) 285
Russo v. New York State Board of Parole,
50 N.Y.2d 69 (1980) 278
Serrano v. Travis, No. 541-03, Slip Op., 9-22-03
(Albany Co.) 282
Silmon v. Travis, 95 N.Y.2d 470, 478 (2000) 282
Stanford v. NYS Div. of Parole, Index No. 1937-09
(Albany Co.2009) 275
Sutherland v. Evans, 82 A.D.3d 1428, 1429 (3d Dept. 2011) ... 278
Thwaites v. NYS Board of Parole, Index No. 5312-11
(Orange Co.2011) 285
Valesquez v. NYS Board of Parole, Index No. 6271-11 221

STATE STATUTES
CPLR Article 78 298
Executive Law §259-(c)(4) 272
Executive Law §259-i[2][c][a] 269
McKinney's Cons. Laws of NY, Book 1, Statutes §54 286

CONSTITUTION
N.Y. Constitution Article I, §6 47
U.S. Constitution 14th Amendment 302

PRELIMINARY STATEMENT

Appellant appeals from a judgment of Supreme Court, Albany County, Hon. _____, J., that denied appellant's C.P.L.R. Article 78 application. Appellant reappeared before the parole board on March 31, 2011 before Commissioner Burns and Commissioner Levy while confined at Livingston Correctional Facility. Appellant utilized the administrative appeal process to challenge the denial of his release to parole supervision. After no response was received, appellant initiated an Article 78 proceeding in Supreme Court, Albany County. The Supreme Court erred when it concluded that appellant was not prejudiced by (1) the parole board's usage of his youthful offender status; (2) the parole board's consideration of inaccurate information included within appellant's parole files; and (3) the parole board's failure to consider all of the statutory factors, combined with the new legislative amendments to the Executive Law that are remedial in nature requires that Appellant be granted a new parole hearing consistent with the new "risk assessment" procedures.

QUESTIONS PRESENTED

Whether the Board of Parole has the authority to deny parole release based upon a youthful offender adjudication?

Whether the Board can continue to consider inaccurate information in Appellant's parole files?

Whether the Parole Board failed to consider all of the statutory factors when making its determination to deny parole release to Appellant?

Whether the remedial amendments to the Executive Law should apply to this Appellate proceeding?

STATEMENT OF THE CASE

A. Background

Appellant is currently serving a sentence of 2 years to 4 years for his conviction for robbery 3°. It was determined by DOCCS that Appellant owed 7 years and 26 days on parole. Appellant's scheduled conditional release date is August 9, 2013 and his maximum expiration date is August 18, 2018.

The guideline range established by the Division of Parole [Community Supervision] had a minimum of 30 months and a maximum of 54 months. A.9. [All pages hereinafter referenced to as A. are a part of the appendix annexed hereto. Mr. _____ was credited with 44 months of total time served when he met with the parole board for rehearing on March 31, 2011.

On March 31, 2011 after appearing before the parole board for his initial appearance and two de novo hearings, appellant reappeared before the parole board for parole release consideration. The Board denied parole and held appellant for the maximum 24 months for the following reasons:

"NOTWITHSTANDING THE EEC, AFTER A REVIEW OF THE RECORD AND INTERVIEW, THE PANEL HAS DETERMINED THAT IF RELEASED AT THIS TIME THERE IS A REASONABLE PROBABILITY THAT YOU WOULD NOT LIVE AND REMAIN AT LIBERTY WITHOUT AGAIN VIOLATING THE LAW AND YOUR RELEASE WOULD BE INCOMPATIBLE WITH THE WELFARE OF SOCIETY. THIS DECISION IS BASED ON THE FOLLOWING FACTORS: YOUR INSTANT OFFENSE IS ROBBERY 3RD IN WHICH YOU ACTED IN CONCERT WITH OTHERS, DISPLAYED WHAT APPEARED TO BE A FIREARM, THREATENED THE VICTIM AND STOLE MONEY AND PROPERTY. YOU COMMITTED THIS OFFENSE WHILE ON PAROLE. YOUR RECORD DATES BACK TO A 1994 ROBBERY 1St, INCLUDES 4 FELONIES, PRIOR PRISON TERMS AND FAILURE AT COMMUNITY SUPERVISION. NOTE IS MADE OF YOUR SENTENCING MINUTES, INSIGHT PROGRAM, DISCIPLINARY RECORD, MERLE COOPER AND ALL OTHER REQUIRED FACTORS. YOU FAILED TO BENEFIT

FROM PRIOR EFFORTS AT REHABILITATION AND REMAIN UNDETERRED BY PRIOR COURT INTERVENTIONS. PAROLE IS DENIED."

(A.8.).

Appellant thereafter filed a timely notice of appeal and submitted briefs to the Division of Parole's Appeals Unit. A.13. After 120 days passed without a decision from the Appeals Unit appellant filed an Article 78 petition in Albany County Court seeking to have the determination of the Board of Parole annulled with a rehearing before a different panel. Said Article 78 petition was denied in a decision and order of Hon. _____, Acting Supreme Court Judge.

B. Inaccurate Information

Appellant's original Inmate Status Report prepared for his initial appearance before the Parole Board indicates that appellant was arrested for burglary 3° on 7/23/07 and that there is no disposition in the case. A.3. In a letter dated March 31, 2011 appellant wrote to the facility parole office at Livingston Correctional Facility informing them that the burglary case was dismissed by the district attorney's office and sealed. In a response dated April 8, 2011 appellant was advised by parole to address the issue via the appeal process or write to the court and ask that a certified disposition be sent to the Inmate Records Coordinator directly. A.15. Appellant then sent letters to counsel for the Division of Parole and the Chairwoman of the Division of Parole informing them of the inaccurate information and requesting that it be expunged from appellant's parole files. Appellant received a response from the facility parole officer informing him that he would have to refer back to their letter dated April 8, 2011 to have the matter handled.[8] A.16-18.

In response to the letters received from parole, appellant wrote to the Kings County Court Clerk seeking a certified disposition of the burglary case. The clerk's office referred appellant to the district attorney's office since they declined prosecution. A.19-20.

Appellant forwarded letters to the Brooklyn district attorney's office and received responses indicating that the arrest for the assault charge was declined, however, parole still refuses to remove the charge from appellant's criminal history even though it is indicated as sealed on his rap sheet. A.14, 21-22.

C. Amendments to Executive Law

According to New York State Executive Law §259-i[2][c][a]:

> "Discretionary release on parole shall not be granted merely as a reward for good conduct or efficient performance

---

[8] The Inmate Status Report prepared for appellant's March 2011 appearance refers back to the original report for appellant's criminal history. Unless it is ordered that this information be expunged it will continue to remain in appellant's files. Therefore, Judicial intervention is necessary.

of duties while confined but after considering if there is a reasonable probability that, if such inmate is released he will live and remain at liberty without violating the law, and that his release is not incompatible with the welfare of society and will not so deprecate the seriousness of his crime as to undermine respect for the law."

In addition to that the statute mandates that the Board follow enumerated factors when making their determination whether the above criteria has been met:

(i) The institutional record including program goals and accomplishments, academic achievements, vocational education, training or work assignments, therapy and interactions with staff and inmates;
(ii) Performance if any, as a participant in a temporary release program;
(iii) Release plans including community resources, employment, education and training and support services available to the inmate;
(iv) Any deportation order issued by the federal government against the inmate while in custody of the department pursuant to section one hundred and forty-seven of the Correction Law.

(v) Any statement made to the Board by the crime victim or the victim's representative, where the crime victim is deceased or mentally or physically incapacitated;

(vi) The length of the determinate sentence to which the inmate would be subject had he or she received a sentence pursuant to section 70.70 or section 70.71 of the penal law for a felony defined in article two hundred twenty or article two hundred twenty-one of the penal law;

(vii) The seriousness of the offense with due consideration to the type of sentence, length of sentence and recommendations of the sentencing court, the district attorney, the attorney for the inmate, the pre-sentencing probation report as well as consideration of any mitigating or aggravating factors, and activities following arrest prior to confinement; and

(viii) Prior criminal record, including the nature and pattern of the offenses, adjustment to any previous probation or parole supervision and institutional confinement.

Andrea Evans, Chairwoman of the Department of Community Supervision, issued a memorandum to the Parole Board dated October 5, 2011 speaking about the amendments to the Executive Law:

"Through the enactment of Chapter 62 of the laws of 2011, Part C, subpart A, 38-(b) Executive Law §259-(c)(4) was amended to provide that the Board of Parole shall:

"Establish written procedures for its use in making Parole Board decisions as required by law. Such written procedures shall incorporate risk and needs principles to measure the rehabilitation of persons appearing before the Board, the likelihood of success of such persons upon release and assist members of the state Board of Parole in determining which inmates may be released to parole supervision.

As you know, members of the Board have been working with staff of the Department of Corrections and Community Supervision in the development of a transitional accountability plan (TAP). This instrument which incorporates risk and needs principles, will provide a meaningful measurement of an inmate's rehabilitation. With respect to the practices of the Boards, the TAP instrument will replace the inmate status report that you have utilized in the past when assessing the appropriateness of an inmate's release to parole supervision. To this end, members of the Board were afforded training in July 2011, in the use of a TAP instrument where it exists. Accordingly, as we proceed, when staff have prepared a TAP instrument for a parole eligible inmate you are to use that document when making your parole release decisions... It is also important to note that the Board was afforded training in September 2011, in the usage of a COMPAS Risk and Needs Assessment tool to understand the interplay between that instrument and the TAP instrument, as well as understanding what each risk levels mean.

Therefore, in your consideration of the statutory criteria set forth in Executive Law §259 — (i)(2)(c)(a)(i) through (viii) you must ascertain what steps an inmate has taken toward their rehabilitation and the likelihood of their success once released to parole release supervision. In this regard any steps taken by an inmate toward effecting their proposed release plans are to be discussed with the inmate during the course of their interview and considered in their deliberations."

In two separate proceedings in Orange County Court it was determined that the 2011 amendments to the Executive Law are remedial in nature, and should therefore be applied retroactively to cases involving appeals of Parole Board Determinations that were still on appeal when the amendments took effect. Thwaites v. NYS Board of Parole, Index No. 5312/2011, (Orange Co.2011); Valesquez v. NYS Board of Parole, Index No. 6271/2011 (Orange Co.2012).

Accordingly, the decision of the Board should be annulled based upon the aforementioned.

ARGUMENT

POINT I

THE PAROLE BOARD'S USAGE OF APPELLANT'S YOUTHFUL OFFENDER ADJUDICATION TO DENY PAROLE RELEASE DEPRIVED APPELLANT OF HIS CONSTITUTIONAL RIGHT TO DUE PROCESS OF LAW AND IS AFFECTED BY IRRATIONALITY BORDERING ON IMPROPRIETY.

In the instant matter, the Parole Board cited "YOUR RECORD DATES BACK TO A 1994 ROBBERY 1ST." As a result of this citation the Parole Board incorrectly referred to appellant's prior youthful offender adjudication as a conviction in violation of his constitutional right to due process.

Appellant's youthful offender adjudication should not have been used as a ground to deny appellant's release to parole supervision. Inasmuch as a youthful offender adjudication is not "a judgment of conviction for a crime or any other offense," the determination of the Parole Board should be annulled. CPL §720.20 and §720.35(1); See Also Matter of Stanford v. NYS Div. of Parole, Albany Co., Supreme Court, Index No. 1937-09, (Connolly,J.), July 8, 2009, citing Matter of Hughes v. NYS Div. of Parole, 21 A.D.3d 1176, 1177 (3rd Dept.2005) ("it is necessary to remand this matter for a rehearing because the Board mistakenly referred to the petitioner's prior youthful offender adjudication as 'a prior conviction.' A youthful offender adjudication is not a judgment of conviction for a crime or other offense."

POINT II

THE PAROLE BOARD'S CONSIDERATION OF INACCURATE INFORMATION RESULTED IN A DENIAL OF PETITIONER'S CONSTITUTIONAL RIGHT TO DUE PROCESS AND IS AFFECTED BY IRRATIONALITY BORDERING ON IMPROPRIETY.

In the 44 months before his reappearance, appellant successfully completed Phase I, Phase II, Phase III, Aggression Replacement Training (A.R.T.), Anger Management, Houses of Healing, Addictions, and the Alcohol Substance and Abuse Treatment (A.S.A.T.) programs. Appellant has also successfully completed the therapeutic Merle Cooper program. Appellant facilitated the Addictions Class, Aggression Replacement Training Class, and worked as a Law Clerk. Appellant has proposed residence with his wife in Syracuse, New York. He also has several letters of reasonable assurance on file for employment and therapeutic programs that are willing to assist him upon his release. Appellant currently works as a Barber and continues to have a supportive family and extended family who have written numerous letters and signed Community Petitions on his behalf.

The parole board's release decisions are governed in part by the release guidelines. In determining the appropriate length of incarceration before parole release, the guidelines consider the seriousness of the instant offense as well as an inmate's prior criminal record. Where, as here, the prior criminal record relied upon contains inaccurate information it cannot be said that appellant received a fair hearing.

The scope of review of a denial of parole release is limited to whether the decision violated a positive statutory requirement or denied a constitutional right, or whether the decision was affected by "irrationality bordering on impropriety." Matter of Russo v. New York State Board of Parole, 50 N.Y.2d 69 (1980).

Here, the Inmate Status Report refers to appellant's criminal history as though appellant has an outstanding charge for burglary 3°. Therefore, in using appellant's criminal history as a reason for its denial of his release to parole supervision, the Board included a case that is sealed and should be expunged from his parole and institutional files.

Appellant avers that the Board relied upon inaccurate information in violation of his right to due process of law as guaranteed under the constitution of this State and the constitution of the United States. This case is distinguished from the case of Matter of Sutherland v. Evans, 82 A.D.3d 1428, 1429 (3rd Dept.2011), where it was discussed at the parole hearing that there was inaccurate information in the record and the Board stated that it would not consider it.

Therefore, since it cannot be concluded on this record that the erroneous information was not utilized by the Board as a basis for its decision to deny appellant parole release the hearing should be annulled and the charge of burglary 3° expunged from appellant's records. N.Y. Constit. Art. I, §6; U.S. Const. 14th Amend.; Lewis v. Travis, 9 A.D.3d 800 (3rd Dept.2004); Burr v. Goord, 283 A.D.2d 891 (3rd Dept.2001).

POINT III

THE PAROLE BOARD IN ITS DECISION FAILED QUALITATIVELY TO DETERMINE WHETHER APPELLANT PRESENTED A CURRENT DANGER TO SOCIETY BASED ON ALL OF THE RELEVANT STATUTORY FACTORS IN ABDICATION OF ITS STATUTORY DUTY.

It is not the role of the Parole Board to resentence appellant according to the personal opinion of its members as to the appropriate penalty for robbery 3°. Here, the sentencing court did not intend for appellant to serve more than the minimum term of 2 years to 4 years. However, appellant has served approximately 5 years thus far. The Board's determination violated the statutory requirements set forth in Executive Law which provides the standards which must be followed by the Board in determining whether to release an inmate to parole supervision.

Petitioner presented the Board with some key endorsements that clearly contradict the Board's determination to deny parole to appellant. Among them is an Inmate Progress Report completed two weeks before appellant's Board appearance by Offender Rehabilitation Coordinator (Counselor) Rogers:

"Has a greater understanding of the group process. Is a commander of information and personalizes those skills and qualities that speak to leadership.

Can speak to large groups and maintain a flow of information keeping the audiences engaged and interacting. Ability to bring insight gathered from own experiences and apply to situations with program.

Mr. _____ is a positive influence amongst his peers."

(A.10.).

The record in this matter demonstrates, unequivocally, appellant's insight into, and unambiguous remorse for the damage that was caused by his criminal acts. Appellant has expressed his guilt and shame with regard to his crimes. This fact relating to appellant's insight is recognized by the Board's denial of parole to appellant. A.8.

B. There is a Strong Rehabilitative Component in the Statute that Requires Consideration.

The Parole Board's decision to deny appellant parole release is a conclusion that he is not rehabilitated. This conclusion is not supported by any factual finding, thereby making it irrational and improper. Executive Law §259-c(4); Friedgood v. NYS Board of Parole, 22 A.D.3d 950, 951.

When the Board is presented with having to weigh the seriousness of the instant offense in determining whether a parole applicant still poses a danger to society, the New York Court of Appeals has reasoned that there is a strong rehabilitative component inherent in the Executive Law that obligates the Board to evaluate appellant's "rehabilitative progress to determine if he still posed a danger..." Silmon v. Travis, 95 N.Y.2d 470, 478 (2000). See Also Matter of Serrano v. Travis, No. 541-03, Slip Op., 9-22-03; (Sup.Ct.Albany Co.) ("the rehabilitative ideal is the cornerstone of indeterminate sentencing").

The Board's determination fails to conform with state law as its decision is conclusory and fails to reveal reasoning. It also fails to explain how and why appellant's instant offense, combined with all the other factors that are required to be considered precludes release for the 4th time in a two year period. Appellant strenuously asserts that if the Board had evaluated appellant's hearing in accordance with the mandates of minimal due process, it would have allowed them to properly evaluate appellant's "rehabilitation" and his "likelihood of success...upon release," based upon who appellant is today rather than who he was approximately 5 years ago when he committed the crime. Especially in light of the Board's comment that "NOTE IS MADE OF SENTENCING MINUTES, INSIGHT PROGRAM." A.8. See Also Memo issued by Andrea Evans, Chairwoman of the New York State Dept, of

Community Supervision ("you must ascertain what steps an inmate has taken toward their rehabilitation and the likelihood of their success once release to parole supervision. In this regard, any steps taken by an inmate toward effecting their rehabilitation, in addition to all aspects of their proposed release plan, are to be discussed with the inmate during the course of their interview and considered in you deliberations") A.24; Silmon v. Travis, 95 N.Y.2d 470 (2000).

Accordingly, the determination of the Board should be annulled.

POINT IV

THE REMEDIAL AMENDMENTS TO EXECUTIVE LAW §259-i[2][c] AND EXECUTIVE LAW §259-c[4] SHOULD BE APPLIED TO THIS PROCEEDING RETROACTIVELY.

In the instant matter, appellant appeared before the Parole Board on March 31, 2011. The amendment to Executive Law §259-i[2][c] became effective on March 31, 2011 and the amendment to Executive Law §259-c[4] became effective on October 1, 2011. Although appellant appeared before the Parole Board prior to the effective date of the statute's amendment, the Division of Parole in reviewing appellant's administrative appeal were required by law to consider the mandatory criteria when making their, determination to reverse affirm, or modify the Board's decision.

The Parole Board's decision to deny appellant parole release is a conclusion that he is not rehabilitated. This conclusion is not supported by any factual finding or any established written procedures, thereby making it improper. Especially in light of the fact that the effective date of Executive Law §259-c had passed and there are no established written procedures in place for the Division to follow even though they failed to review the appeal as required by law.

The legislative intent behind the addition of §259-c[4] to the Executive Law in 2011 is to require the Parole Board to evaluate incarcerated individuals; "rehabilitation" and their "likelihood of success... upon release," based upon who they are today, as opposed to the person they were years ago when they committed their crime. Professor Phillip M. Genty, Columbia Law School, Changes to Parole Laws Signal Potentially Sweeping Policy Shift, NYLJ, September 1, 2011.

In Matter of Thwaites v. NYS Board of Parole, NY Slip Op. 21453 (Orange Co.2011), Justice Ecker stated that the Parole Board, in denying Thwaites release to parole supervision, relied on "past focused rhetoric, not future-focused risk assessment analysis." The court directed that the Parole Board afford Mr. Thwaites a new parole hearing wherein the rehabilitation factor is applied retroactively due to the remedial nature of the new risk assessment procedures.

Since the amendments to the Executive Law are remedial and "remedial statutes have been regarded as an exception to any general rule against retroactivity," this honorable Court should conclude that the remedial amendments apply in this pending proceeding. Gleason v. Vee, 96 N.Y.2d 117, 122 (2001) ("it is axiomatic that remedial legislation should be given retroactive effect in order to effectuate its beneficial purpose"); Majewski

v. Broadalbin-Perth Cent. School District, 91 N.Y.2d 577 (1998); McKinney's Cons. Laws of NY, Book 1, Statutes §54.

CONCLUSION

WHEREFORE, appellant respectfully prays that this Court enter an Order; annulling respondent's determination to hold a parole hearing that failed to review each of the applicable factors mandated for consideration; and Directing respondent to hold a de novo hearing in front of a different panel in which the Board must fairly consider each of the applicable factors mandated, including the new risk assessment procedures and the rehabilitation factor, together with such other and further relief which this Court deems just and proper.

Dated: _____ ____, 20__ .
_____, New York

Respectfully submitted,

_____ # _____
Appellant Pro Se
_____ Correctional Facility

_____ NY _____

Sworn to before me this
_____ day of _____ 20___ .

THE COURT OF APPEALS

The Court of Appeals is New York's highest State Court. There are four appellate division departments in the State of New York and they are all bound to follow decisions handed down by the Court of Appeals. The Court of Appeals was established by the State's Constitution Article VI, §2 in 1846. There are seven judges including a Chief Judge who are all appointed by the Governor, and must be confirmed by the New York Senate. Once they are chosen they sit on the bench of the Court for a term of 14 years.

Appealing a case to the Court of Appeals is a little more complicated than appealing to the appellate division. In a headline published in the New York Law Journal on November 27, 2009, it was reported that "through October, judges on the Court of Appeals had granted leave in 68 criminal cases, already the most in any calendar year this decade." The Court of Appeals granted leave to appeal in a little over 3 percent of the time in 2009, as opposed to granting leave 1.8 percent of the time since 1996. Although the number of applications granted has increased, the numbers are small in comparison to the amount of applications filed with the Court.

Criminal cases are not the only kinds of cases that are considered by the Court of Appeals. Civil cases are also considered. In 2005, only 6.3 percent of leave applications were granted. Between the years of 2001-05, 7.24 percent were granted. The majority of leave applications filed by, or on behalf of prisoners will be criminal in relation to their direct case or postconviction motion, or civil in regard to a state habeas corpus proceeding or article 78 proceeding.

A leave to appeal application must be made to the Court of Appeals within 30 days after the decision you are appealing was served upon the applicant. All of the issues included in the application must have been properly preserved. Meaning that they must have been raised each and every step of the way to give each tribunal a fair opportunity to address the issues. Once a lower court has refused to entertain an issue due to a failure to properly preserve it, the Court of Appeals will refuse to review it as well. In that regard, if you plan on taking your issue(s) all the way, make sure that you include everything from the start.

Federal courts will also refuse to entertain an issue that was not properly presented or preserved in the state courts. With this in mind, even though you are raising certain issues on a state level first, always include your constitutional issues, cases and citations in your arguments from the beginning. It makes it easier for you doing it this way because you really don't have to change much besides the format at the next level.

APPEALS TO THE COURT OF APPEALS AS OF RIGHT

Appeals to the Court of Appeals as of right are governed in New York by the Civil Practice Law and Rules (CPLR) §5601. The only appeals "as of right" to the Court of Appeals are:

(a) Dissent- If there is a dissent by at least two judges in The Appellate Division which has made the final determination on a question of law in favor of the party taking the appeal in an action that originated in an administrative agency, supreme court, family court, county court, surrogates court, or the court of claims.

(b) Constitutional grounds:
1. A final order of an Appellate Division which directly involves the construction of the State Constitution or the United States Constitution.
2. From a final determination of an action of a court of record of original instance which involves a question of the validity of a state statute or federal statute under New York State's Constitution or the Constitution of the United States.

(c) From an order granting new trial or hearing, upon stipulation for a judgment absolute- A judgment from a case originating in one of the courts mentioned above or an administrative agency which resulted in a "new trial order." This is not a good vehicle for an appellant because it is unpredictable and can result in an appellant losing everything. Especially in the case of a lawsuit settlement.

(d) Based upon nonfinal determination of Appellate Division- These types of cases usually involve orders of the Appellate Division that decided some issues but lacked finality because other issues were still pending before a lower court. Once the lower court rules on the issues, the appellant had the option of bypassing the Appellate Division and bringing their issues directly before the Court of Appeals. However, the appellant would be limited to only raising the issues that were previously decided by the appellate court.

If the appellant wants these issues to be heard by the Court of Appeals they can ask that their leave application be "held in abeyance" until they have exhausted the claims just passed on by the lower tribunal. If permission is granted they will have the opportunity to exhaust these claims before the Appellate Division and then raise all of their issues together before the Court of Appeals. Otherwise they can waive appellate review of the issues that were not passed on by the Appellate Division and proceed with only the issues that were properly preserved.

Article VI, §3 of the New York State Constitution provides that "appeals as of right" may also be taken from a court of original jurisdiction where the judgment is of death (death penalty case). In the case of People v. Lavalle, 3 N.Y.3d 88, 783 N.Y.S.2d 485 (2005), the Court of Appeals modified a death sentence and concluded that under the present statute, "the death penalty may not be imposed." This was due to their determination that the deadlock instruction included in Criminal Procedure Law (CPL) §400.27(10) created the risk of coercing jurors into sentencing a criminal defendant to death in violation of the state' due process clause. As a result of this ruling, no death penalty cases can go forward in New York State until the legislature enacts a new statute that is in compliance with a criminal defendant's right to due process of law.

The Court of Appeals usually hears appeals four times more in civil cases than in criminal cases in a year. In civil cases a large number of leave applications are granted by Appellate Division judges. The Court of Appeals will also grant civil leave if at least two out of seven judges approve the application.

MOTIONS FOR LEAVE TO APPEAL

WHICH COURT?

An application for a certificate granting leave to appeal to the Court of Appeals can be made to either a judge of the appellate court that made the order you are appealing from, or to a judge of the Court of Appeals. In the event that the appeal is from an order of an intermediate appellate court, the application must be made to a judge of the Court of Appeals.

WHEN TO FILE

An appellant must seek leave to appeal to the Court of Appeals within 30 days after receipt of the Appellate Division's order they are appealing from.

WHAT TO FILE

Criminal Leave Applications

Leave to appeal applications in a criminal case are made to the Chief Judge pursuant to CPL §460.20 in the form of a letter, with proof of service upon the adverse party (usually the district attorney) sent to the attention of the clerk of the court, Court of Appeals, 20 Eagle Street, Albany, New York, 12207.

The letter shall include the names of all co-defendants, the status of their appeals, if known, that no application for the same relief has been made to a justice of the appellate division, and whether an oral hearing on the application in person or by telephone conference call is requested. *Always consult with your appellate attorney (if you have one) before filing a leave application on your own. If you file an application before your attorney does, their application will be barred. No judge can consider a second application. People v. Nelson, 55 N.Y.2d 743, 447 N.Y.S.2d 155 (1981).

In the case of People v. Liner, 70 N.Y.2d 945, 524 N.Y.S.2d 573 (1988), the Court held that it could not entertain defense counsel's CPL §460.20 application after the defendant had submitted his own pro se application to a justice of the appellate division.

Civil Leave Applications

Leave to appeal applications in civil cases shall consist of an original and six (6) copies of the leave application signed by the attorney or the self-represented litigant. Copies of all orders and opinions rendered below, if the appendix method was used, and also one copy of the briefs filed by each party.

Two copies of the leave application must be filed upon the other party with one "proof of service" filed in the Court indicating that the two copies were served on the other party. An application to proceed as a poor person can also be filed with the Court. We have provided a Sample Civil Leave Application which pertains to the issue of a prisoner appealing an adverse parole board hearing decision that was also denied by the Appellate Division, Third Department. We have also provided a blank Poor Person Application.

WHAT TO EXPECT AFTER YOU FILE

Once you file your leave application with the Court and serve it on the other party you can expect for the other party to respond with a memorandum of law in opposition to your motion for leave to appeal. In the opposing party's papers they will no doubt be stating that the lower court's decision that denied your relief was proper based on the same reasoning that the lower court used to deny your appeal. If your appellate lawyer has filed the leave application on your behalf in a criminal case and your application is granted, they should then ask to be assigned to represent you on the appeal due to their familiarity of your case. However, there is no right to counsel in a criminal matter once you have exhausted your direct appeal. So be careful to make sure that the lawyer who handles your case has filed a leave application within the 30 day period or you will be time barred.

There is also no right to counsel in civil appeals. Although you are asking for one to represent your case, if none is assigned then you must proceed on your own. If you are granted leave to appeal you will have 60 days from that date to perfect the appeal by submitting your briefs and appendix. You will be expected to file an original and 24 copies of the appendix and brief if leave is granted. The upper right hand of the brief should contain a notation stating that the case will be submitted since you cannot perform an oral argument on your behalf in the court. If you cannot afford to provide the court with the copies you can ask the court for permission to allow you to proceed with fewer copies required, and on the original record which the Court of Appeals clerk can obtain from the Appellate Division. Three (3) copies of the brief Must be served on the other party with the original proof of service of three (3) copies upon the other party forwarded to the court. You do not have to provide the other party with the appendix (exhibits). For a complete listing of what the Court of Appeals requires you should consult "Rules of the Court of Appeals of the State of New York, Part 500." See Also 22 NYCRR §500.

It is not required that you submit a Reply Brief after you receive a response. However, if you choose to submit a Reply Brief for consideration you must do so within fifteen (15) days after the respondent's brief was served upon you. You will have to submit an original and 24 copies of your Reply Brief to the Court along with proof of service of 3 copies having been served on the other party. Unless, of course you get permission from the court to file less than the required amount due to your indigency (poor person status).

In the event that you are not successful, the next step will be to take your issue(s) to federal court. In a lot of situations the Court of Appeals will not give you the relief you seek due to its prior precedents. There is a legal term called "stare decisis" or "let the ruling stand." This means that a court, such as the Court of Appeals will give deference to its prior decisions and will not disturb them unless you can persuade them to change their prior ruling. This is what setting precedents is all about. Always look for arguments that can show a court why a prior decision should not be followed anymore if your issue is contrary to the precedent.

STATE OF NEW YORK
COURT OF APPEALS
_____

In the Matter of _____, #_____

                    Appellant,

v.

_____, as COMMISSIONER OF THE
DEPARTMENT OF CORRECTIONS

                    Respondent.

Albany Co.
Index No. _____
A.D. No. _____

MOTION FOR LEAVE TO APPEAL
_____

                  (SAMPLE)
              NOTICE OF MOTION

    PLEASE TAKE NOTICE, that upon the papers attached hereto, the Plaintiff-Appellant _____ will move this Court at the Court of appeals Hall, 20 Eagle Street, Albany, New York, on the _____ day of _____, 20___ at 9:00 a.m. for an Order, pursuant to CPLR §5602(a)(1)(i), for leave to appeal to the Court of Appeals from an Opinion and Order of the Appellate Division, Third Department, decided and

entered _____ _____,
20___.

PLEASE TAKE FURTHER NOTICE, that pursuant to Rule 500.11(a) and 22 NYCRR §500.11(a) of this Court, the within motion will be submitted on the papers herein and that your personal appearance in opposition to the motion is neither required nor permitted.

PLEASE TAKE FURTHER NOTICE, that answering affidavits and memoranda, if any, are required to be filed with the Court and served upon the undersigned pro se petitioner pursuant to Rule 500.11(a), and (d)(2), and 22 NYCRR §500.11(a), (d)(2) of the Court of Appeals.

Dated: _____ ____, 20___.

Respectfully submitted,

_____
_____ # _____
Appellant Pro Se
_____ Corr. Facility

_____
_____ NY _____

TO: _____
Attorney General of the
State of New York
Attorney for Respondent
Department of Law
The Capitol
Albany, NY 12224

CONCISE STATEMENT OF QUESTIONS PRESENTED FOR REVIEW

QUESTION:

Should leave to appeal be granted by this Court where: (1) the Appellate Division, Third Department has determined that DOCCS did not err in calculating petitioner's 1999 sentence to run consecutively with his undischarged sentences when it is contrary to clearly established federal law as determined by the United States Supreme Court?

ANSWER:

Because the Third Department's decision is in conflict with the Constitution as interpreted by the United States Supreme Court and the Supremacy Clause, review is merited by this Court and clarification pursuant to Rule 500.11(d)(1)(v), for the purpose of uniformity on these important issues of Civil Practice in the State of New York.

PROCEDURAL HISTORY OF THE CASE

Plaintiff-Movant _____ seeks leave to appeal from an Opinion and Order of the Appellate Division, Third Judicial Department decided and entered on _____ _____, 20___, A-7., which affirmed an Order of the Supreme Court, Albany County (_____, j.), entered _____ _____, 20___, dismissing petitioner's CPLR Article 78 petition, A-1. The Appellate Division for the Third Department's decision is based on case law that is in conflict with the United States Constitution and the Supremacy Clause. In the proceedings below, petitioner asked the lower Court and respondent "whether DOCCS has the authority to calculate petitioner's 1999 sentence as running consecutively to his prior undischarged sentences without express directive from the sentencing court when it is contrary to clearly established federal law that is binding upon New York Courts?" Hill v. United States ex rel. Wampler, 298 U.S. 460, 465 (1936). Respondent failed to answer petitioner's constitutional questions and sought answers shrouded in New York law. The Appellate Division's decision also did not answer the questions of constitutional magnitude that were presented below when petitioner clearly cited decisions in the United States Supreme Court. A-14.

The Appellate Division's Order was served upon plaintiff by regular mail with a letter dated _____ _____, 20___, A-5. This motion for leave to appeal and the proposed appeal which was served upon counsel for respondent by regular mail within thirty (30) days (plus five days for mailing) after service of the Appellate Division Order, is therefore timely pursuant to CPLR §5513.

JURISDICTION OF THE MOTION FOR LEAVE TO APPEAL

This Court has jurisdiction over the current motion for leave to appeal pursuant to CPLR §5602(a)(1)(i). This action originated in the Supreme Court and the final order appealed from determines the action pursuant to CPLR §5611.

STATEMENT OF FACTS

On October 6, 2009 petitioner was sentenced by (Hon. Judge's Name) of Kings County Supreme Court as a persistent felony offender to an indeterminate term of 20 years to life for robbery 1°.

At the time such sentence was imposed, petitioner still owed time on a prior undischarged term of 2 years to 4 years, and another prior undischarged term of 3½ years to 7 years. A1-19.

Specifically, petitioner had served approximately 6½ years of those terms under imprisonment, and DOCCS' failure to calculate his time as concurrent has increased the time he is to serve his minimum by 6½ years.

The sentencing court failed to specify and indicate whether the current sentence imposed upon petitioner was to run concurrently with or consecutively to the prior undischarged term, and DOCCS officials took it upon themselves to decide to run the sentences consecutively and compute petitioner's release dates accordingly.

After thoroughly exhausting his administrative remedies regarding DOCCS' consecutive calculation of his undischarged terms, appellant filed a petition pursuant to Article 78 of the Civil Practice Law and Rules. Said petition was denied by (Hon. Judge's Name), Supreme Court, Albany County, on April 7, 2010. Petitioner filed a timely notice of appeal to the Appellate Division, Third Department. In a Decision and Order dated June 8, 2010 the Appellate Division for the Third Department granted appellant's application for permission to proceed as a poor person and time to perfect appeal was extended to August 3, 2010. In an Order decided and entered October 5, 2010 the Appellate Division for the Third Department affirmed the Supreme Court's decision. A-32.

ARGUMENT

LEAVE TO APPEAL SHOULD BE GRANTED TO RESOLVE THE CONFLICT BETWEEN THE THIRD DEPARTMENT'S DECISION THAT DOCCS DOES NOT ERR IN CALCULATING THE SENTENCES TO RUN CONSECUTIVELY EVEN IN THE ABSENCE OF AN EXPLICIT DIRECTION FROM THE SENTENCING COURT TO DO SO BECAUSE IT IS CONTRARY TO DECISIONS OF THE UNITED STATES SUPREME COURT AND OTHER APPELLATE DECISIONS IN FEDERAL COURTS APPLYING NEW YORK LAW.

In the instant matter, the Appellate Division for the Third Judicial Department held that "DOCCS does not err in calculating the sentences to run concurrently even in the absence of an explicit direction from the sentencing court to do so."

The decision of the Third Department is in direct conflict with the United States Supreme Court and the Second Circuit Court of Appeals. Therefore, it is imperative that this Court grant leave to appeal in this case to clarify whether it is unconstitutional for DOCCS to calculate sentences to run consecutively even in the absence of an explicit direction from the sentencing court to do so when the United States Supreme Court has already ruled on the subject over 70 years ago.

In the case of Hill v. United States ex rel. Wampler, 298 U.S. 460 (1936), the

United States Supreme Court held that: "[T]he sentence imposed by a sentencing judge is controlling; it is this sentence that constitutes the court's judgment and authorizes custody of the defendant."

Earley v. Murray, 451 F.3d 71 (2d Cir.2006), cert, denied, 551 U.S. _____, 127 S.Ct. 3014 (2007) (Mem)., relied substantially on Wampler to hold that the additional imposition of post relief supervision upon a defendant by DOCCS was unlawful as it violated the defendant's constitutional rights and moreover, that the additional provisions of PRS imposed by DOCS is a nullity."

Appellant posits that the decision in Wampler is binding on New York State Courts through the Fourteenth Amendment and the Supremacy Clause. Therefore, this Court should resolve the conflict regarding the unanswered question of whether the authority of Wampler is controlling on this issue, and whether this "split" between New York Law and the Supreme Law of the Land should be resolved to prevent a manifest injustice.

CONCLUSION

For all of the foregoing reasons, appellant respectfully requests that this Court issue an Order granting appellant's motion for leave to appeal, bringing up for review all issues raised in the Appellate Division, together with such other and further relief as to the Court may seem just and proper.

Dated: _____ _____, 20___.

> _____
> _____ # _____
> Appellant Pro Se
> _____ Correctional Facility
>
> _____
> _____ NY _____

Sworn to before me this
_____ day of _____ 20___.

_____

COURT OF APPEALS
STATE OF NEW YORK
--X
In the Matter of _____, #_____

    Petitioner-Appellant, **NOTICE OF MOTION FOR PERMISSION TO PROCEED AS A POOR PERSON**

             v.

_____, as Commissioner of the New York State Department of Corrections,

Index No. _____

A.D. No. _____

Respondent.
--X

SIRS:

    PLEASE TAKE NOTICE, that upon the affidavit of _____ _____, sworn to on the _____ day of _____, 20___, and upon all of the papers and proceedings held previously, a motion will be made to this Court to be held in the Court of Appeals Hall located in the City of Albany, New York, on the _____ day of _____, 20___, at 9:00 a.m. or as soon thereafter as counsel may be heard for an Order permitting the appellant to proceed as a poor person in the above entitled action upon the ground that said defendant has insufficient income and property to pay the costs, fees, and expenses of the above entitled action, and for such other and further relief as may be just, proper, and equitable.

The above entitled action is brought for _____.

Pursuant to CPLR §2214(b), answering affidavits, if any, are required to be served upon the undersigned at least seven days before the return date of this motion.

Dated: _____ _____, 20____.

        Yours etc.,

        _____
        _____ # _____
        Appellant Pro Se
        _____ Correctional Facility

        _____
        _____ NY _____

COURT OF APPEALS
STATE OF NEW YORK
--X
In the Matter of _____, #_____

Petitioner-Appellant,

                              AFFIDAVIT IN SUPPORT
                              OF MOTION TO PROCEED
      v.   **AS A POOR PERSON**

_____, as Commissioner of the
New York State Department of Index No. _____
Corrections,

                                A.D. No. _____
            Respondent.
--X
STATE OF NEW YORK)
)ss.:
COUNTY OF _____)

_____, being duly sworn, deposes and says:

    1. I am the appellant in the above entitled action and make this affidavit in support of my motion requesting permission to proceed as a poor person.

    2. That I am currently incarcerated at the _____ Correctional Facility, County of _____, State of New York.

    3. I am an incarcerated person and have no other income than my institutional weekly pay of $_____ per week, the only other property that I have is my personal property.

4. I have no other assets in the form of real property, stocks, bonds, bank accounts or savings accounts.

5. I am unable to pay the costs, fees and expenses necessary to prosecute the above entitled action.

6. The above entitled action is brought by me against the above named respondent for the following grounds:

_____
_____
_____
_____

7. No other person has any beneficial interest in the above entitled action.

8. No previous application for the relief sought herein prayed for has been made.

WHEREFORE, appellant respectfully asks that an order issue pursuant to CPLR §1101 granting him/her permission to proceed as a poor person in the above entitled action and the assigning of an attorney for the prosecution of the above entitled action.

                Yours etc.,

                _____
                _____ # _____
                Appellant Pro Se
                _____ Correctional Facility
                _____
                _____ NY _____

Sworn to before me this
_____ day of _____ 20____.

_____

Made in the USA
Columbia, SC
02 April 2024